C-4601 CAREER EXAMINATION SERIES

*This is your
PASSBOOK for...*

Teachers' Retirement Examiner

*Test Preparation Study Guide
Questions & Answers*

NLC®

NATIONAL LEARNING CORPORATION®

COPYRIGHT NOTICE

This book is SOLELY intended for, is sold ONLY to, and its use is RESTRICTED to individual, bona fide applicants or candidates who qualify by virtue of having seriously filed applications for appropriate license, certificate, professional and/or promotional advancement, higher school matriculation, scholarship, or other legitimate requirements of education and/or governmental authorities.

This book is NOT intended for use, class instruction, tutoring, training, duplication, copying, reprinting, excerption, or adaptation, etc., by:

1) Other publishers
2) Proprietors and/or Instructors of "Coaching" and/or Preparatory Courses
3) Personnel and/or Training Divisions of commercial, industrial, and governmental organizations
4) Schools, colleges, or universities and/or their departments and staffs, including teachers and other personnel
5) Testing Agencies or Bureaus
6) Study groups which seek by the purchase of a single volume to copy and/or duplicate and/or adapt this material for use by the group as a whole without having purchased individual volumes for each of the members of the group
7) Et al.

Such persons would be in violation of appropriate Federal and State statutes.

PROVISION OF LICENSING AGREEMENTS – Recognized educational, commercial, industrial, and governmental institutions and organizations, and others legitimately engaged in educational pursuits, including training, testing, and measurement activities, may address request for a licensing agreement to the copyright owners, who will determine whether, and under what conditions, including fees and charges, the materials in this book may be used them. In other words, a licensing facility exists for the legitimate use of the material in this book on other than an individual basis. However, it is asseverated and affirmed here that the material in this book CANNOT be used without the receipt of the express permission of such a licensing agreement from the Publishers. Inquiries re licensing should be addressed to the company, attention rights and permissions department.

All rights reserved, including the right of reproduction in whole or in part, in any form or by any means, electronic or mechanical, including photocopying, recording, or by any information storage and retrieval system, without permission in writing from the Publisher.

Copyright © 2024 by
National Learning Corporation

212 Michael Drive, Syosset, NY 11791
(516) 921-8888 • www.passbooks.com
E-mail: info@passbooks.com

PASSBOOK® SERIES

THE *PASSBOOK® SERIES* has been created to prepare applicants and candidates for the ultimate academic battlefield – the examination room.

At some time in our lives, each and every one of us may be required to take an examination – for validation, matriculation, admission, qualification, registration, certification, or licensure.

Based on the assumption that every applicant or candidate has met the basic formal educational standards, has taken the required number of courses, and read the necessary texts, the *PASSBOOK® SERIES* furnishes the one special preparation which may assure passing with confidence, instead of failing with insecurity. Examination questions – together with answers – are furnished as the basic vehicle for study so that the mysteries of the examination and its compounding difficulties may be eliminated or diminished by a sure method.

This book is meant to help you pass your examination provided that you qualify and are serious in your objective.

The entire field is reviewed through the huge store of content information which is succinctly presented through a provocative and challenging approach – the question-and-answer method.

A climate of success is established by furnishing the correct answers at the end of each test.

You soon learn to recognize types of questions, forms of questions, and patterns of questioning. You may even begin to anticipate expected outcomes.

You perceive that many questions are repeated or adapted so that you can gain acute insights, which may enable you to score many sure points.

You learn how to confront new questions, or types of questions, and to attack them confidently and work out the correct answers.

You note objectives and emphases, and recognize pitfalls and dangers, so that you may make positive educational adjustments.

Moreover, you are kept fully informed in relation to new concepts, methods, practices, and directions in the field.

You discover that you are actually taking the examination all the time: you are preparing for the examination by "taking" an examination, not by reading extraneous and/or supererogatory textbooks.

In short, this PASSBOOK®, used directedly, should be an important factor in helping you to pass your test.

TEACHERS' RETIREMENT EXAMINER

DUTIES

As a Teachers' Retirement Examiner, you would, under the supervision of a higher-level examiner, determine membership eligibility and calculate benefit amounts paid to Teachers' Retirement System members and claimants. Tasks include reviewing applications to determine eligibility for benefits, calculating amount of benefits due, preparing vouchers for payment of benefits, and notifying claimants of determinations. You would be expected to communicate with members of the Teachers' Retirement System and their families, representatives from other retirement systems, school districts, and attorneys to provide information both by telephone and in writing. You may also be expected to assign work to and review the work of lower level clerical staff.

SCOPE OF THE EXAMINATION

The written test is designed to test for knowledge, skills, and/or abilities in such areas as:

1. **Arithmetic reasoning** - These questions test your ability to solve an arithmetic problem presented in sentence or short paragraph form. You must read the problem, understand the situation presented, decide what must be done to solve it, and apply the appropriate arithmetic operation(s) in the appropriate order, in order to determine the correct answer. Knowledge of addition, subtraction, multiplication, and division will be necessary. Questions may also involve the use of percents, decimals, and fractions.

2. **Preparing written material** - These questions test for the ability to present information clearly and accurately, and to organize paragraphs logically and comprehensibly. For some questions, you will be given information in two or three sentences followed by four restate ments of the information. You must then choose the best version. For other questions, you will be given paragraphs with their sentences out of order. You must then choose, from four suggestions, the best order for the sentences.

3. **Public contact principles and practices** - These questions test for the ability to interact with other people, to gather and present information, and to provide assistance, advice, and effective customer service in a courteous and professional manner. Questions will cover such topics as understanding and responding to people with diverse needs, perspectives, personalities, and levels of familiarity with agency operations, as well as acting in a way that both serves the public and reflects well on your agency.

4. **Understanding and interpreting written material** - These questions test how well you comprehend written material. You will be provided with brief reading selections and will be asked questions about the selections. All the information required to answer the questions will be presented in the selections; you will not be required to have any special knowledge relating to the subject areas of the selections.

HOW TO TAKE A TEST

I. YOU MUST PASS AN EXAMINATION

A. *WHAT EVERY CANDIDATE SHOULD KNOW*

Examination applicants often ask us for help in preparing for the written test. What can I study in advance? What kinds of questions will be asked? How will the test be given? How will the papers be graded?

As an applicant for a civil service examination, you may be wondering about some of these things. Our purpose here is to suggest effective methods of advance study and to describe civil service examinations.

Your chances for success on this examination can be increased if you know how to prepare. Those "pre-examination jitters" can be reduced if you know what to expect. You can even experience an adventure in good citizenship if you know why civil service exams are given.

B. *WHY ARE CIVIL SERVICE EXAMINATIONS GIVEN?*

Civil service examinations are important to you in two ways. As a citizen, you want public jobs filled by employees who know how to do their work. As a job seeker, you want a fair chance to compete for that job on an equal footing with other candidates. The best-known means of accomplishing this two-fold goal is the competitive examination.

Exams are widely publicized throughout the nation. They may be administered for jobs in federal, state, city, municipal, town or village governments or agencies.

Any citizen may apply, with some limitations, such as the age or residence of applicants. Your experience and education may be reviewed to see whether you meet the requirements for the particular examination. When these requirements exist, they are reasonable and applied consistently to all applicants. Thus, a competitive examination may cause you some uneasiness now, but it is your privilege and safeguard.

C. *HOW ARE CIVIL SERVICE EXAMS DEVELOPED?*

Examinations are carefully written by trained technicians who are specialists in the field known as "psychological measurement," in consultation with recognized authorities in the field of work that the test will cover. These experts recommend the subject matter areas or skills to be tested; only those knowledges or skills important to your success on the job are included. The most reliable books and source materials available are used as references. Together, the experts and technicians judge the difficulty level of the questions.

Test technicians know how to phrase questions so that the problem is clearly stated. Their ethics do not permit "trick" or "catch" questions. Questions may have been tried out on sample groups, or subjected to statistical analysis, to determine their usefulness.

Written tests are often used in combination with performance tests, ratings of training and experience, and oral interviews. All of these measures combine to form the best-known means of finding the right person for the right job.

II. HOW TO PASS THE WRITTEN TEST

A. NATURE OF THE EXAMINATION

To prepare intelligently for civil service examinations, you should know how they differ from school examinations you have taken. In school you were assigned certain definite pages to read or subjects to cover. The examination questions were quite detailed and usually emphasized memory. Civil service exams, on the other hand, try to discover your present ability to perform the duties of a position, plus your potentiality to learn these duties. In other words, a civil service exam attempts to predict how successful you will be. Questions cover such a broad area that they cannot be as minute and detailed as school exam questions.

In the public service similar kinds of work, or positions, are grouped together in one "class." This process is known as *position-classification*. All the positions in a class are paid according to the salary range for that class. One class title covers all of these positions, and they are all tested by the same examination.

B. FOUR BASIC STEPS

1) Study the announcement

How, then, can you know what subjects to study? Our best answer is: "Learn as much as possible about the class of positions for which you've applied." The exam will test the knowledge, skills and abilities needed to do the work.

Your most valuable source of information about the position you want is the official exam announcement. This announcement lists the training and experience qualifications. Check these standards and apply only if you come reasonably close to meeting them.

The brief description of the position in the examination announcement offers some clues to the subjects which will be tested. Think about the job itself. Review the duties in your mind. Can you perform them, or are there some in which you are rusty? Fill in the blank spots in your preparation.

Many jurisdictions preview the written test in the exam announcement by including a section called "Knowledge and Abilities Required," "Scope of the Examination," or some similar heading. Here you will find out specifically what fields will be tested.

2) Review your own background

Once you learn in general what the position is all about, and what you need to know to do the work, ask yourself which subjects you already know fairly well and which need improvement. You may wonder whether to concentrate on improving your strong areas or on building some background in your fields of weakness. When the announcement has specified "some knowledge" or "considerable knowledge," or has used adjectives like "beginning principles of..." or "advanced ... methods," you can get a clue as to the number and difficulty of questions to be asked in any given field. More questions, and hence broader coverage, would be included for those subjects which are more important in the work. Now weigh your strengths and weaknesses against the job requirements and prepare accordingly.

3) Determine the level of the position

Another way to tell how intensively you should prepare is to understand the level of the job for which you are applying. Is it the entering level? In other words, is this the position in which beginners in a field of work are hired? Or is it an intermediate or advanced level? Sometimes this is indicated by such words as "Junior" or "Senior" in the class title. Other jurisdictions use Roman numerals to designate the level – Clerk I, Clerk II, for example. The word "Supervisor" sometimes appears in the title. If the level is not indicated by the title, check the description of duties. Will you be working under very close supervision, or will you have responsibility for independent decisions in this work?

4) Choose appropriate study materials

Now that you know the subjects to be examined and the relative amount of each subject to be covered, you can choose suitable study materials. For beginning level jobs, or even advanced ones, if you have a pronounced weakness in some aspect of your training, read a modern, standard textbook in that field. Be sure it is up to date and has general coverage. Such books are normally available at your library, and the librarian will be glad to help you locate one. For entry-level positions, questions of appropriate difficulty are chosen – neither highly advanced questions, nor those too simple. Such questions require careful thought but not advanced training.

If the position for which you are applying is technical or advanced, you will read more advanced, specialized material. If you are already familiar with the basic principles of your field, elementary textbooks would waste your time. Concentrate on advanced textbooks and technical periodicals. Think through the concepts and review difficult problems in your field.

These are all general sources. You can get more ideas on your own initiative, following these leads. For example, training manuals and publications of the government agency which employs workers in your field can be useful, particularly for technical and professional positions. A letter or visit to the government department involved may result in more specific study suggestions, and certainly will provide you with a more definite idea of the exact nature of the position you are seeking.

III. KINDS OF TESTS

Tests are used for purposes other than measuring knowledge and ability to perform specified duties. For some positions, it is equally important to test ability to make adjustments to new situations or to profit from training. In others, basic mental abilities not dependent on information are essential. Questions which test these things may not appear as pertinent to the duties of the position as those which test for knowledge and information. Yet they are often highly important parts of a fair examination. For very general questions, it is almost impossible to help you direct your study efforts. What we can do is to point out some of the more common of these general abilities needed in public service positions and describe some typical questions.

1) General information

Broad, general information has been found useful for predicting job success in some kinds of work. This is tested in a variety of ways, from vocabulary lists to questions about current events. Basic background in some field of work, such as sociology or economics, may be sampled in a group of questions. Often these are principles which have become familiar to most persons through exposure rather than through formal training. It is difficult to advise you how to study for these questions; being alert to the world around you is our best suggestion.

2) Verbal ability

An example of an ability needed in many positions is verbal or language ability. Verbal ability is, in brief, the ability to use and understand words. Vocabulary and grammar tests are typical measures of this ability. Reading comprehension or paragraph interpretation questions are common in many kinds of civil service tests. You are given a paragraph of written material and asked to find its central meaning.

3) Numerical ability

Number skills can be tested by the familiar arithmetic problem, by checking paired lists of numbers to see which are alike and which are different, or by interpreting charts and graphs. In the latter test, a graph may be printed in the test booklet which you are asked to use as the basis for answering questions.

4) Observation

A popular test for law-enforcement positions is the observation test. A picture is shown to you for several minutes, then taken away. Questions about the picture test your ability to observe both details and larger elements.

5) Following directions

In many positions in the public service, the employee must be able to carry out written instructions dependably and accurately. You may be given a chart with several columns, each column listing a variety of information. The questions require you to carry out directions involving the information given in the chart.

6) Skills and aptitudes

Performance tests effectively measure some manual skills and aptitudes. When the skill is one in which you are trained, such as typing or shorthand, you can practice. These tests are often very much like those given in business school or high school courses. For many of the other skills and aptitudes, however, no short-time preparation can be made. Skills and abilities natural to you or that you have developed throughout your lifetime are being tested.

Many of the general questions just described provide all the data needed to answer the questions and ask you to use your reasoning ability to find the answers. Your best preparation for these tests, as well as for tests of facts and ideas, is to be at your physical and mental best. You, no doubt, have your own methods of getting into an exam-taking mood and keeping "in shape." The next section lists some ideas on this subject.

IV. KINDS OF QUESTIONS

Only rarely is the "essay" question, which you answer in narrative form, used in civil service tests. Civil service tests are usually of the short-answer type. Full instructions for answering these questions will be given to you at the examination. But in case this is your first experience with short-answer questions and separate answer sheets, here is what you need to know:

1) Multiple-choice Questions

Most popular of the short-answer questions is the "multiple choice" or "best answer" question. It can be used, for example, to test for factual knowledge, ability to solve problems or judgment in meeting situations found at work.

A multiple-choice question is normally one of three types—
- It can begin with an incomplete statement followed by several possible endings. You are to find the one ending which *best* completes the statement, although some of the others may not be entirely wrong.
- It can also be a complete statement in the form of a question which is answered by choosing one of the statements listed.

- It can be in the form of a problem – again you select the best answer.

Here is an example of a multiple-choice question with a discussion which should give you some clues as to the method for choosing the right answer:

When an employee has a complaint about his assignment, the action which will *best* help him overcome his difficulty is to
   A. discuss his difficulty with his coworkers
   B. take the problem to the head of the organization
   C. take the problem to the person who gave him the assignment
   D. say nothing to anyone about his complaint

In answering this question, you should study each of the choices to find which is best. Consider choice "A" – Certainly an employee may discuss his complaint with fellow employees, but no change or improvement can result, and the complaint remains unresolved. Choice "B" is a poor choice since the head of the organization probably does not know what assignment you have been given, and taking your problem to him is known as "going over the head" of the supervisor. The supervisor, or person who made the assignment, is the person who can clarify it or correct any injustice. Choice "C" is, therefore, correct. To say nothing, as in choice "D," is unwise. Supervisors have and interest in knowing the problems employees are facing, and the employee is seeking a solution to his problem.

2) True/False Questions

The "true/false" or "right/wrong" form of question is sometimes used. Here a complete statement is given. Your job is to decide whether the statement is right or wrong.

SAMPLE: A roaming cell-phone call to a nearby city costs less than a non-roaming call to a distant city.

This statement is wrong, or false, since roaming calls are more expensive.

This is not a complete list of all possible question forms, although most of the others are variations of these common types. You will always get complete directions for answering questions. Be sure you understand *how* to mark your answers – ask questions until you do.

V. RECORDING YOUR ANSWERS

Computer terminals are used more and more today for many different kinds of exams.
For an examination with very few applicants, you may be told to record your answers in the test booklet itself. Separate answer sheets are much more common. If this separate answer sheet is to be scored by machine – and this is often the case – it is highly important that you mark your answers correctly in order to get credit.
An electronic scoring machine is often used in civil service offices because of the speed with which papers can be scored. Machine-scored answer sheets must be marked with a pencil, which will be given to you. This pencil has a high graphite content which responds to the electronic scoring machine. As a matter of fact, stray dots may register as answers, so do not let your pencil rest on the answer sheet while you are pondering the correct answer. Also, if your pencil lead breaks or is otherwise defective, ask for another.

Since the answer sheet will be dropped in a slot in the scoring machine, be careful not to bend the corners or get the paper crumpled.

The answer sheet normally has five vertical columns of numbers, with 30 numbers to a column. These numbers correspond to the question numbers in your test booklet. After each number, going across the page are four or five pairs of dotted lines. These short dotted lines have small letters or numbers above them. The first two pairs may also have a "T" or "F" above the letters. This indicates that the first two pairs only are to be used if the questions are of the true-false type. If the questions are multiple choice, disregard the "T" and "F" and pay attention only to the small letters or numbers.

Answer your questions in the manner of the sample that follows:

32. The largest city in the United States is
   A. Washington, D.C.
   B. New York City
   C. Chicago
   D. Detroit
   E. San Francisco

1) Choose the answer you think is best. (New York City is the largest, so "B" is correct.)
2) Find the row of dotted lines numbered the same as the question you are answering. (Find row number 32)
3) Find the pair of dotted lines corresponding to the answer. (Find the pair of lines under the mark "B.")
4) Make a solid black mark between the dotted lines.

VI. BEFORE THE TEST

Common sense will help you find procedures to follow to get ready for an examination. Too many of us, however, overlook these sensible measures. Indeed, nervousness and fatigue have been found to be the most serious reasons why applicants fail to do their best on civil service tests. Here is a list of reminders:

- Begin your preparation early – Don't wait until the last minute to go scurrying around for books and materials or to find out what the position is all about.
- Prepare continuously – An hour a night for a week is better than an all-night cram session. This has been definitely established. What is more, a night a week for a month will return better dividends than crowding your study into a shorter period of time.
- Locate the place of the exam – You have been sent a notice telling you when and where to report for the examination. If the location is in a different town or otherwise unfamiliar to you, it would be well to inquire the best route and learn something about the building.
- Relax the night before the test – Allow your mind to rest. Do not study at all that night. Plan some mild recreation or diversion; then go to bed early and get a good night's sleep.
- Get up early enough to make a leisurely trip to the place for the test – This way unforeseen events, traffic snarls, unfamiliar buildings, etc. will not upset you.
- Dress comfortably – A written test is not a fashion show. You will be known by number and not by name, so wear something comfortable.

- Leave excess paraphernalia at home – Shopping bags and odd bundles will get in your way. You need bring only the items mentioned in the official notice you received; usually everything you need is provided. Do not bring reference books to the exam. They will only confuse those last minutes and be taken away from you when in the test room.
- Arrive somewhat ahead of time – If because of transportation schedules you must get there very early, bring a newspaper or magazine to take your mind off yourself while waiting.
- Locate the examination room – When you have found the proper room, you will be directed to the seat or part of the room where you will sit. Sometimes you are given a sheet of instructions to read while you are waiting. Do not fill out any forms until you are told to do so; just read them and be prepared.
- Relax and prepare to listen to the instructions
- If you have any physical problem that may keep you from doing your best, be sure to tell the test administrator. If you are sick or in poor health, you really cannot do your best on the exam. You can come back and take the test some other time.

VII. AT THE TEST

The day of the test is here and you have the test booklet in your hand. The temptation to get going is very strong. Caution! There is more to success than knowing the right answers. You must know how to identify your papers and understand variations in the type of short-answer question used in this particular examination. Follow these suggestions for maximum results from your efforts:

1) Cooperate with the monitor

The test administrator has a duty to create a situation in which you can be as much at ease as possible. He will give instructions, tell you when to begin, check to see that you are marking your answer sheet correctly, and so on. He is not there to guard you, although he will see that your competitors do not take unfair advantage. He wants to help you do your best.

2) Listen to all instructions

Don't jump the gun! Wait until you understand all directions. In most civil service tests you get more time than you need to answer the questions. So don't be in a hurry. Read each word of instructions until you clearly understand the meaning. Study the examples, listen to all announcements and follow directions. Ask questions if you do not understand what to do.

3) Identify your papers

Civil service exams are usually identified by number only. You will be assigned a number; you must not put your name on your test papers. Be sure to copy your number correctly. Since more than one exam may be given, copy your exact examination title.

4) Plan your time

Unless you are told that a test is a "speed" or "rate of work" test, speed itself is usually not important. Time enough to answer all the questions will be provided, but this does not mean that you have all day. An overall time limit has been set. Divide the total time (in minutes) by the number of questions to determine the approximate time you have for each question.

5) Do not linger over difficult questions

If you come across a difficult question, mark it with a paper clip (useful to have along) and come back to it when you have been through the booklet. One caution if you do this – be sure to skip a number on your answer sheet as well. Check often to be sure that you have not lost your place and that you are marking in the row numbered the same as the question you are answering.

6) Read the questions

Be sure you know what the question asks! Many capable people are unsuccessful because they failed to *read* the questions correctly.

7) Answer all questions

Unless you have been instructed that a penalty will be deducted for incorrect answers, it is better to guess than to omit a question.

8) Speed tests

It is often better NOT to guess on speed tests. It has been found that on timed tests people are tempted to spend the last few seconds before time is called in marking answers at random – without even reading them – in the hope of picking up a few extra points. To discourage this practice, the instructions may warn you that your score will be "corrected" for guessing. That is, a penalty will be applied. The incorrect answers will be deducted from the correct ones, or some other penalty formula will be used.

9) Review your answers

If you finish before time is called, go back to the questions you guessed or omitted to give them further thought. Review other answers if you have time.

10) Return your test materials

If you are ready to leave before others have finished or time is called, take ALL your materials to the monitor and leave quietly. Never take any test material with you. The monitor can discover whose papers are not complete, and taking a test booklet may be grounds for disqualification.

VIII. EXAMINATION TECHNIQUES

1) Read the general instructions carefully. These are usually printed on the first page of the exam booklet. As a rule, these instructions refer to the timing of the examination; the fact that you should not start work until the signal and must stop work at a signal, etc. If there are any *special* instructions, such as a choice of questions to be answered, make sure that you note this instruction carefully.

2) When you are ready to start work on the examination, that is as soon as the signal has been given, read the instructions to each question booklet, underline any key words or phrases, such as *least, best, outline, describe* and the like. In this way you will tend to answer as requested rather than discover on reviewing your paper that you *listed without describing*, that you selected the *worst* choice rather than the *best* choice, etc.

3) If the examination is of the objective or multiple-choice type – that is, each question will also give a series of possible answers: A, B, C or D, and you are called upon to select the best answer and write the letter next to that answer on your answer paper – it is advisable to start answering each question in turn. There may be anywhere from 50 to 100 such questions in the three or four hours allotted and you can see how much time would be taken if you read through all the questions before beginning to answer any. Furthermore, if you come across a question or group of questions which you know would be difficult to answer, it would undoubtedly affect your handling of all the other questions.

4) If the examination is of the essay type and contains but a few questions, it is a moot point as to whether you should read all the questions before starting to answer any one. Of course, if you are given a choice – say five out of seven and the like – then it is essential to read all the questions so you can eliminate the two that are most difficult. If, however, you are asked to answer all the questions, there may be danger in trying to answer the easiest one first because you may find that you will spend too much time on it. The best technique is to answer the first question, then proceed to the second, etc.

5) Time your answers. Before the exam begins, write down the time it started, then add the time allowed for the examination and write down the time it must be completed, then divide the time available somewhat as follows:
    - If 3-1/2 hours are allowed, that would be 210 minutes. If you have 80 objective-type questions, that would be an average of 2-1/2 minutes per question. Allow yourself no more than 2 minutes per question, or a total of 160 minutes, which will permit about 50 minutes to review.
    - If for the time allotment of 210 minutes there are 7 essay questions to answer, that would average about 30 minutes a question. Give yourself only 25 minutes per question so that you have about 35 minutes to review.

6) The most important instruction is to *read each question* and make sure you know what is wanted. The second most important instruction is to *time yourself properly* so that you answer every question. The third most important instruction is to *answer every question*. Guess if you have to but include something for each question. Remember that you will receive no credit for a blank and will probably receive some credit if you write something in answer to an essay question. If you guess a letter – say "B" for a multiple-choice question – you may have guessed right. If you leave a blank as an answer to a multiple-choice question, the examiners may respect your feelings but it will not add a point to your score. Some exams may penalize you for wrong answers, so in such cases *only*, you may not want to guess unless you have some basis for your answer.

7) Suggestions
    a. Objective-type questions
        1. Examine the question booklet for proper sequence of pages and questions
        2. Read all instructions carefully
        3. Skip any question which seems too difficult; return to it after all other questions have been answered
        4. Apportion your time properly; do not spend too much time on any single question or group of questions

5. Note and underline key words – *all, most, fewest, least, best, worst, same, opposite,* etc.
6. Pay particular attention to negatives
7. Note unusual option, e.g., unduly long, short, complex, different or similar in content to the body of the question
8. Observe the use of "hedging" words – *probably, may, most likely,* etc.
9. Make sure that your answer is put next to the same number as the question
10. Do not second-guess unless you have good reason to believe the second answer is definitely more correct
11. Cross out original answer if you decide another answer is more accurate; do not erase until you are ready to hand your paper in
12. Answer all questions; guess unless instructed otherwise
13. Leave time for review

b. Essay questions
1. Read each question carefully
2. Determine exactly what is wanted. Underline key words or phrases.
3. Decide on outline or paragraph answer
4. Include many different points and elements unless asked to develop any one or two points or elements
5. Show impartiality by giving pros and cons unless directed to select one side only
6. Make and write down any assumptions you find necessary to answer the questions
7. Watch your English, grammar, punctuation and choice of words
8. Time your answers; don't crowd material

8) Answering the essay question

Most essay questions can be answered by framing the specific response around several key words or ideas. Here are a few such key words or ideas:

M's: manpower, materials, methods, money, management
P's: purpose, program, policy, plan, procedure, practice, problems, pitfalls, personnel, public relations

a. Six basic steps in handling problems:
1. Preliminary plan and background development
2. Collect information, data and facts
3. Analyze and interpret information, data and facts
4. Analyze and develop solutions as well as make recommendations
5. Prepare report and sell recommendations
6. Install recommendations and follow up effectiveness

b. Pitfalls to avoid
1. *Taking things for granted* – A statement of the situation does not necessarily imply that each of the elements is necessarily true; for example, a complaint may be invalid and biased so that all that can be taken for granted is that a complaint has been registered

2. *Considering only one side of a situation* – Wherever possible, indicate several alternatives and then point out the reasons you selected the best one
3. *Failing to indicate follow up* – Whenever your answer indicates action on your part, make certain that you will take proper follow-up action to see how successful your recommendations, procedures or actions turn out to be
4. *Taking too long in answering any single question* – Remember to time your answers properly

IX. AFTER THE TEST

Scoring procedures differ in detail among civil service jurisdictions although the general principles are the same. Whether the papers are hand-scored or graded by machine we have described, they are nearly always graded by number. That is, the person who marks the paper knows only the number – never the name – of the applicant. Not until all the papers have been graded will they be matched with names. If other tests, such as training and experience or oral interview ratings have been given, scores will be combined. Different parts of the examination usually have different weights. For example, the written test might count 60 percent of the final grade, and a rating of training and experience 40 percent. In many jurisdictions, veterans will have a certain number of points added to their grades.

After the final grade has been determined, the names are placed in grade order and an eligible list is established. There are various methods for resolving ties between those who get the same final grade – probably the most common is to place first the name of the person whose application was received first. Job offers are made from the eligible list in the order the names appear on it. You will be notified of your grade and your rank as soon as all these computations have been made. This will be done as rapidly as possible.

People who are found to meet the requirements in the announcement are called "eligibles." Their names are put on a list of eligible candidates. An eligible's chances of getting a job depend on how high he stands on this list and how fast agencies are filling jobs from the list.

When a job is to be filled from a list of eligibles, the agency asks for the names of people on the list of eligibles for that job. When the civil service commission receives this request, it sends to the agency the names of the three people highest on this list. Or, if the job to be filled has specialized requirements, the office sends the agency the names of the top three persons who meet these requirements from the general list.

The appointing officer makes a choice from among the three people whose names were sent to him. If the selected person accepts the appointment, the names of the others are put back on the list to be considered for future openings.

That is the rule in hiring from all kinds of eligible lists, whether they are for typist, carpenter, chemist, or something else. For every vacancy, the appointing officer has his choice of any one of the top three eligibles on the list. This explains why the person whose name is on top of the list sometimes does not get an appointment when some of the persons lower on the list do. If the appointing officer chooses the second or third eligible, the No. 1 eligible does not get a job at once, but stays on the list until he is appointed or the list is terminated.

X. HOW TO PASS THE INTERVIEW TEST

The examination for which you applied requires an oral interview test. You have already taken the written test and you are now being called for the interview test – the final part of the formal examination.

You may think that it is not possible to prepare for an interview test and that there are no procedures to follow during an interview. Our purpose is to point out some things you can do in advance that will help you and some good rules to follow and pitfalls to avoid while you are being interviewed.

What is an interview supposed to test?

The written examination is designed to test the technical knowledge and competence of the candidate; the oral is designed to evaluate intangible qualities, not readily measured otherwise, and to establish a list showing the relative fitness of each candidate – as measured against his competitors – for the position sought. Scoring is not on the basis of "right" and "wrong," but on a sliding scale of values ranging from "not passable" to "outstanding." As a matter of fact, it is possible to achieve a relatively low score without a single "incorrect" answer because of evident weakness in the qualities being measured.

Occasionally, an examination may consist entirely of an oral test – either an individual or a group oral. In such cases, information is sought concerning the technical knowledges and abilities of the candidate, since there has been no written examination for this purpose. More commonly, however, an oral test is used to supplement a written examination.

Who conducts interviews?

The composition of oral boards varies among different jurisdictions. In nearly all, a representative of the personnel department serves as chairman. One of the members of the board may be a representative of the department in which the candidate would work. In some cases, "outside experts" are used, and, frequently, a businessman or some other representative of the general public is asked to serve. Labor and management or other special groups may be represented. The aim is to secure the services of experts in the appropriate field.

However the board is composed, it is a good idea (and not at all improper or unethical) to ascertain in advance of the interview who the members are and what groups they represent. When you are introduced to them, you will have some idea of their backgrounds and interests, and at least you will not stutter and stammer over their names.

What should be done before the interview?

While knowledge about the board members is useful and takes some of the surprise element out of the interview, there is other preparation which is more substantive. It *is* possible to prepare for an oral interview – in several ways:

1) Keep a copy of your application and review it carefully before the interview

This may be the only document before the oral board, and the starting point of the interview. Know what education and experience you have listed there, and the sequence and dates of all of it. Sometimes the board will ask you to review the highlights of your experience for them; you should not have to hem and haw doing it.

2) Study the class specification and the examination announcement

Usually, the oral board has one or both of these to guide them. The qualities, characteristics or knowledges required by the position sought are stated in these documents. They offer valuable clues as to the nature of the oral interview. For example, if the job involves supervisory responsibilities, the announcement will usually indicate that knowledge of modern supervisory methods and the qualifications of the candidate as a supervisor will be tested. If so, you can expect such questions, frequently in the form of a hypothetical situation which you are expected to solve. NEVER go into an oral without knowledge of the duties and responsibilities of the job you seek.

3) Think through each qualification required

Try to visualize the kind of questions you would ask if you were a board member. How well could you answer them? Try especially to appraise your own knowledge and background in each area, *measured against the job sought*, and identify any areas in which you are weak. Be critical and realistic – do not flatter yourself.

4) Do some general reading in areas in which you feel you may be weak

For example, if the job involves supervision and your past experience has NOT, some general reading in supervisory methods and practices, particularly in the field of human relations, might be useful. Do NOT study agency procedures or detailed manuals. The oral board will be testing your understanding and capacity, not your memory.

5) Get a good night's sleep and watch your general health and mental attitude

You will want a clear head at the interview. Take care of a cold or any other minor ailment, and of course, no hangovers.

What should be done on the day of the interview?

Now comes the day of the interview itself. Give yourself plenty of time to get there. Plan to arrive somewhat ahead of the scheduled time, particularly if your appointment is in the fore part of the day. If a previous candidate fails to appear, the board might be ready for you a bit early. By early afternoon an oral board is almost invariably behind schedule if there are many candidates, and you may have to wait. Take along a book or magazine to read, or your application to review, but leave any extraneous material in the waiting room when you go in for your interview. In any event, relax and compose yourself.

The matter of dress is important. The board is forming impressions about you – from your experience, your manners, your attitude, and your appearance. Give your personal appearance careful attention. Dress your best, but not your flashiest. Choose conservative, appropriate clothing, and be sure it is immaculate. This is a business interview, and your appearance should indicate that you regard it as such. Besides, being well groomed and properly dressed will help boost your confidence.

Sooner or later, someone will call your name and escort you into the interview room. *This is it.* From here on you are on your own. It is too late for any more preparation. But remember, you asked for this opportunity to prove your fitness, and you are here because your request was granted.

What happens when you go in?

The usual sequence of events will be as follows: The clerk (who is often the board stenographer) will introduce you to the chairman of the oral board, who will introduce you to the other members of the board. Acknowledge the introductions before you sit down. Do not be surprised if you find a microphone facing you or a stenotypist sitting by. Oral interviews are usually recorded in the event of an appeal or other review.

Usually the chairman of the board will open the interview by reviewing the highlights of your education and work experience from your application – primarily for the benefit of the other members of the board, as well as to get the material into the record. Do not interrupt or comment unless there is an error or significant misinterpretation; if that is the case, do not hesitate. But do not quibble about insignificant matters. Also, he will usually ask you some question about your education, experience or your present job – partly to get you to start talking and to establish the interviewing "rapport." He may start the actual questioning, or turn it over to one of the other members. Frequently, each member undertakes the questioning on a particular area, one in which he is perhaps most competent, so you can expect each member to participate in the examination. Because time is limited, you may also expect some rather abrupt switches in the direction the questioning takes, so do not be upset by it. Normally, a board member will not pursue a single line of questioning unless he discovers a particular strength or weakness.

After each member has participated, the chairman will usually ask whether any member has any further questions, then will ask you if you have anything you wish to add. Unless you are expecting this question, it may floor you. Worse, it may start you off on an extended, extemporaneous speech. The board is not usually seeking more information. The question is principally to offer you a last opportunity to present further qualifications or to indicate that you have nothing to add. So, if you feel that a significant qualification or characteristic has been overlooked, it is proper to point it out in a sentence or so. Do not compliment the board on the thoroughness of their examination – they have been sketchy, and you know it. If you wish, merely say, "No thank you, I have nothing further to add." This is a point where you can "talk yourself out" of a good impression or fail to present an important bit of information. Remember, *you close the interview yourself*.

The chairman will then say, "That is all, Mr. _____, thank you." Do not be startled; the interview is over, and quicker than you think. Thank him, gather your belongings and take your leave. Save your sigh of relief for the other side of the door.

How to put your best foot forward

Throughout this entire process, you may feel that the board individually and collectively is trying to pierce your defenses, seek out your hidden weaknesses and embarrass and confuse you. Actually, this is not true. They are obliged to make an appraisal of your qualifications for the job you are seeking, and they want to see you in your best light. Remember, they must interview all candidates and a non-cooperative candidate may become a failure in spite of their best efforts to bring out his qualifications. Here are 15 suggestions that will help you:

1) Be natural – Keep your attitude confident, not cocky

If you are not confident that you can do the job, do not expect the board to be. Do not apologize for your weaknesses, try to bring out your strong points. The board is interested in a positive, not negative, presentation. Cockiness will antagonize any board member and make him wonder if you are covering up a weakness by a false show of strength.

2) Get comfortable, but don't lounge or sprawl

Sit erectly but not stiffly. A careless posture may lead the board to conclude that you are careless in other things, or at least that you are not impressed by the importance of the occasion. Either conclusion is natural, even if incorrect. Do not fuss with your clothing, a pencil or an ashtray. Your hands may occasionally be useful to emphasize a point; do not let them become a point of distraction.

3) Do not wisecrack or make small talk

This is a serious situation, and your attitude should show that you consider it as such. Further, the time of the board is limited – they do not want to waste it, and neither should you.

4) Do not exaggerate your experience or abilities

In the first place, from information in the application or other interviews and sources, the board may know more about you than you think. Secondly, you probably will not get away with it. An experienced board is rather adept at spotting such a situation, so do not take the chance.

5) If you know a board member, do not make a point of it, yet do not hide it

Certainly you are not fooling him, and probably not the other members of the board. Do not try to take advantage of your acquaintanceship – it will probably do you little good.

6) Do not dominate the interview

Let the board do that. They will give you the clues – do not assume that you have to do all the talking. Realize that the board has a number of questions to ask you, and do not try to take up all the interview time by showing off your extensive knowledge of the answer to the first one.

7) Be attentive

You only have 20 minutes or so, and you should keep your attention at its sharpest throughout. When a member is addressing a problem or question to you, give him your undivided attention. Address your reply principally to him, but do not exclude the other board members.

8) Do not interrupt

A board member may be stating a problem for you to analyze. He will ask you a question when the time comes. Let him state the problem, and wait for the question.

9) Make sure you understand the question

Do not try to answer until you are sure what the question is. If it is not clear, restate it in your own words or ask the board member to clarify it for you. However, do not haggle about minor elements.

10) Reply promptly but not hastily

A common entry on oral board rating sheets is "candidate responded readily," or "candidate hesitated in replies." Respond as promptly and quickly as you can, but do not jump to a hasty, ill-considered answer.

11) Do not be peremptory in your answers

A brief answer is proper – but do not fire your answer back. That is a losing game from your point of view. The board member can probably ask questions much faster than you can answer them.

12) Do not try to create the answer you think the board member wants

He is interested in what kind of mind you have and how it works – not in playing games. Furthermore, he can usually spot this practice and will actually grade you down on it.

13) Do not switch sides in your reply merely to agree with a board member

Frequently, a member will take a contrary position merely to draw you out and to see if you are willing and able to defend your point of view. Do not start a debate, yet do not surrender a good position. If a position is worth taking, it is worth defending.

14) Do not be afraid to admit an error in judgment if you are shown to be wrong

The board knows that you are forced to reply without any opportunity for careful consideration. Your answer may be demonstrably wrong. If so, admit it and get on with the interview.

15) Do not dwell at length on your present job

The opening question may relate to your present assignment. Answer the question but do not go into an extended discussion. You are being examined for a *new* job, not your present one. As a matter of fact, try to phrase ALL your answers in terms of the job for which you are being examined.

Basis of Rating

Probably you will forget most of these "do's" and "don'ts" when you walk into the oral interview room. Even remembering them all will not ensure you a passing grade. Perhaps you did not have the qualifications in the first place. But remembering them will help you to put your best foot forward, without treading on the toes of the board members.

Rumor and popular opinion to the contrary notwithstanding, an oral board wants you to make the best appearance possible. They know you are under pressure – but they also want to see how you respond to it as a guide to what your reaction would be under the pressures of the job you seek. They will be influenced by the degree of poise you display, the personal traits you show and the manner in which you respond.

ABOUT THIS BOOK

This book contains tests divided into Examination Sections. Go through each test, answering every question in the margin. We have also attached a sample answer sheet at the back of the book that can be removed and used. At the end of each test look at the answer key and check your answers. On the ones you got wrong, look at the right answer choice and learn. Do not fill in the answers first. Do not memorize the questions and answers, but understand the answer and principles involved. On your test, the questions will likely be different from the samples. Questions are changed and new ones added. If you understand these past questions you should have success with any changes that arise. Tests may consist of several types of questions. We have additional books on each subject should more study be advisable or necessary for you. Finally, the more you study, the better prepared you will be. This book is intended to be the last thing you study before you walk into the examination room. Prior study of relevant texts is also recommended. NLC publishes some of these in our Fundamental Series. Knowledge and good sense are important factors in passing your exam. Good luck also helps. So now study this Passbook, absorb the material contained within and take that knowledge into the examination. Then do your best to pass that exam.

EXAMINATION SECTION

EXAMINATION SECTION
TEST 1

DIRECTIONS: Each question or incomplete statement is followed by several suggested answers or completions. Select the one that BEST answers the question or completes the statement. *PRINT THE LETTER OF THE CORRECT ANSWER IN THE SPACE AT THE RIGHT.*

NOTE: The term member as used in this test refers to a member of the employees' retirement system.

1. If a member had pension deductions of $717.60 this year and his bi-weekly salary was $480, the rate of his pension contribution was

   A. 5.60% B. 5.65% C. 5.70% D. 5.75%

2. If the amount of a cost-of-living increase paid to retirees in 1982 was $75.80 and this amount has increased at a rate of 5 percent annually thereafter, then the cost-of-living increase paid in 1987 would be MOST NEARLY

   A. $92.11 B. $94.75 C. $96.71 D. $98.54

3. If a prospective retiree's salary is $12,350 per annum and she earned 15% additional pay during her last year of service because of overtime, the total earnings for that year would be

   A. $12,967.50 B. $13,679.40 C. $14,202.50 D. $14,225.20

4. A member whose salary is $258.80 per week and whose pension rate is 8% makes an annual contribution to the retirement system of

   A. $907.40 B. $1,066.70 C. $1,076.60 D. $2,070.40

5. If a member's salary is $235.00 per week and he contributes to the retirement system at the rate of 7% of his salary per week, his contribution for the year is

   A. $651.30 B. $855.40 C. $858.76 D. $886.76

6. A member who earns a bi-weekly salary of $295.70 and whose pension rate is 6% makes an annual contribution to the retirement system of

   A. $425.80 B. $461.29 C. $851.60 D. $922.58

7. Suppose that, on January 1 of one year, a member's account had a deficit of $1,000. The deficit was discovered on January 1, two years later, and on that date the member was notified that he owed the retirement system $1,081.60, of which $81.60 was interest. The annual rate of interest charged to this member's account was

   A. 4.0% B. 4.1% C. 8.1% D. 8.6%

8. If a member makes yearly pension contributions totalling $615.55 and her rate of contribution is 6.5%, the member's yearly salary is

   A. $9,070.40 B. $9,470.00 C. $9,704.00 D. $10,239.23

9. Suppose that a member earns a yearly salary of $10,848 and contributes to the retirement system at a rate of 8%. This member's monthly contribution is

   A. $71.23   B. $72.32   C. $73.23   D. $74.53

10. If a member earns $13,540 annually and contributes $974.88 a year to the retirement system, his rate of contribution is

    A. 6.5%   B. 6.8%   C. 7.0%   D. 7.2%

11. If 27.6% of an employee's salary is withheld for taxes and the employee earns $18,346.00 a year, the amount withheld totals

    A. $4,898.38   B. $4,922.41   C. $5,063.50   D. $5,088.34

12. If a member earns $8,940.00 a year and contributes $52.15 a month to the retirement system, the rate at which this member contributes to the system is

    A. 7.0%   B. 7.2%   C. 7.6%   D. 8.0%

13. If a member who earns a salary of $15,245.00 a year has a pension contribution rate of 7.6%, the member's pension contributions for the year total

    A. $1,021.41   B. $1,146.58   C. $1,158.62   D. $1,518.62

14. If an employee receives weekly paychecks of $167.38, $171.42, $165.56, and $170.84 during a four-week period, his average weekly salary for that period is

    A. $168.80   B. $171.70   C. $174.30   D. $178.70

15. In a three-month period, an employee's gross salary was $2,628.75, including pay for overtime totalling $175.80 the first month, $159.30 the second month, and $182.40 the third month.
    Without overtime pay, the employee's average monthly gross salary during the three-month period was

    A. $698.35   B. $703.75   C. $716.95   D. $876.25

16. Mr. Pearce, a member, has been paying back a loan which he borrowed from his funds in the retirement system, at the rate of $12.60 every two weeks.
    After twelve weeks, how much money will he have paid back on the loan, disregarding interest?

    A. $37.50   B. $75.60   C. $76.50   D. $151.20

17. If a member makes a bi-weekly pension payment of $34.82, after sixteen weeks the member's payments will total

    A. $278.56   B. $287.65   C. $472.53   D. $557.12

18. If a retiree receives advance pension payments of $978.56, $1,328.94, $1,459.23, and $2,007.01, he has been paid a total of

    A. $4,773.74   B. $5,773.74   C. $5,973.74   D. $15,773.74

19. A member whose annual earnings three years prior to retirement were $14,876.96, $12,994.53, and $13,709.74 earned an average annual income for those years of   19._____

    A. $13,860.41
    B. $14,580.23
    C. $15,526.41
    D. $41,580.23

20. Suppose that Mr. Jones receives a weekly salary of $229.83, before deductions. He is currently paying back a loan of $1,500 which he took from his pension funds, through weekly payroll deductions of $8.47.   20._____
    If his other fixed deductions amount to $53.65 weekly, how much pay would Mr. Jones take home over a period of 28 weeks?

    A. $4,695.88   B. $4,933.04   C. $6,198.08   D. $6,435.24

KEY (CORRECT ANSWERS)

1.	D	11.	C
2.	C	12.	A
3.	C	13.	C
4.	C	14.	A
5.	B	15.	B
6.	B	16.	B
7.	A	17.	A
8.	B	18.	B
9.	B	19.	A
10.	D	20.	A

TEST 2

DIRECTIONS: Each question or incomplete statement is followed by several suggested answers or completions. Select the one that BEST answers the question or completes the statement. *PRINT THE LETTER OF THE CORRECT ANSWER IN THE SPACE AT THE RIGHT.*

NOTE: *The term member as used in this test refers to a member of the employees' retirement system.*

1. The formula for computing base salary is: Earnings equals base gross plus additional gross.
   If an employee's earnings during a particular period are in the amounts of $597.45, $535.92. $639.91, and $552.83, and his base gross salary is $525.50 per paycheck, what is the total of the additional gross earned by the employee during that period?

   A. $224.11 B. $224.21 C. $224.51 D. $244.11

2. If a lump sum benefit is paid by the retirement system in an amount equal to 3/7 of an employee's last yearly salary of $13,486.50, the amount of the death benefit paid is MOST NEARLY

   A. $5,749.29 B. $5,759.92 C. $5,779.92 D. $5,977.29

3. Suppose that a member has paid fifteen installments on a 28-installment loan.
   The percentage of the number of installments paid to the retirement system is

   A. 53.57% B. 53.97% C. 54.57% D. 55.37%

4. If an employee takes a one-month vacation during a calendar year, the percentage of the year during which he works is MOST NEARLY

   A. 90.9% B. 91.3% C. 91.6% D. 92.1%

5. Suppose that an employee took a leave of absence totalling seven months during a calendar year.
   Assuming the employee did not take any vacation time during the remainder of that year, the percentage of the year in which he worked is MOST NEARLY

   A. 41.7% B. 43.3% C. 46.5% D. 47.1%

6. A member has borrowed $4,725 from her funds in the retirement system.
   If $3,213 has been repaid, the percentage of the loan which is still outstanding is MOST NEARLY

   A. 16% B. 32% C. 48% D. 68%

7. If an employee worked only 24 weeks during the year because of illness, the portion of the year he was out of work was MOST NEARLY

   A. 46% B. 48% C. 51% D. 54%

8. If an employee purchased credit for a sixteen-week period of service which he had prior to rejoining the retirement system, the percentage of a year he purchased credit for was MOST NEARLY

   A. 27.9% B. 28.8% C. 30.7% D. 33.3%

1.__
2.__
3.__
4.__
5.__
6.__
7.__
8.__

9. If an employee contributes 2/11 of his yearly salary to his pension fund account, the percentage of his yearly salary which he contributes is MOST NEARLY

   A. 17.9%   B. 18.2%   C. 18.4%   D. 19.0%

10. In 1975, the maximum amount of income from which social security tax could be withheld (base salary) was $14,100. In 1977, the base salary was $16,500.
    The 1977 base salary represents a percentage increase over the 1975 base salary of

    A. 15%   B. 16%   C. 17%   D. 18%

11. If 17.5% of an employee's salary is withheld for taxes, the one of the following which is the fraction of the salary withheld is

    A. 3/20   B. 8/35   C. 7/40   D. 4/25

12. If a person withdraws 42% of the funds from his account with the retirement system, the remaining balance represents a fraction of MOST NEARLY

    A. 7/13   B. 5/9   C. 7/12   D. 4/7

13. An examiner may compute the advance pension payment due to a prospective retiree by using the following formula: 1.2% x number of years of service x last year's salary. Using this formula, the amount of the advance payment due to an employee who joined the retirement system on January 30, 1965 and retired on February 1, 1987, with a yearly salary of $12,090, is MOST NEARLY

    A. $2,981.67   B. $3,092.75   C. $3,191.76   D. $3,375.84

Questions 14-15.

DIRECTIONS: Answer Questions 14 and 15 on the basis of the following information. Assume that 328 disability retirement applications were processed this year, of which 242 were ordinary disability retirements and the balance were accident disability retirements.

14. Based upon the information given above, this year the percentage of disability retirement applications processed which were ordinary disability retirements was MOST NEARLY

    A. 69%   B. 72%   C. 74%   D. 76%

15. Based upon the information given above, if 3/5 of all ordinary disability retirement applications and 3/4 of all accident disability retirement applications were for males, then the number of female disability retirees was MOST NEARLY

    A. 97   B. 118   C. 131   D. 145

16. The amount of an employee's annual annuity benefit may be determined by dividing the amount the employee has in her annuity savings fund by the applicable annuity factor. Based on the foregoing information, if an employee's annual annuity benefit has been determined to be $5,730 and the applicable annuity factor is 9.65, the amount this employee has in her annuity savings fund is

    A. $54,778.80   B. $54,987.30
    C. $55,294.50   D. $59,378.23

17. A member who has paid twenty semi-monthly payments of her yearly pension contribution of $473.00 has paid a total of

   A. $390.58   B. $391.75   C. $393.30   D. $394.16

17.____

18. Suppose that an employee's monthly pension benefit is computed by dividing 3/5 of his final year's salary by 12.
   If an employee retires after earning $9,500 in his final year, his monthly pension benefit will be

   A. $420.00   B. $425.00   C. $445.00   D. $475.00

18.____

Question 19.

DIRECTIONS: Answer Question 19 SOLELY on the basis of the information in the paragraph below.

Upon retirement for service, a member shall receive a retirement allowance which shall consist of an annuity which shall be the actuarial equivalent of his accumulated deductions at the time of his retirement, and a pension, in addition to his annuity, which shall be equal to one service-fraction of his final compensation, multiplied by the number of years of service since he last became a member credited to him, and a pension which is the actuarial equivalent of the reserve-for-increased-take-home-pay to which he may then be entitled, if any.

19. According to the above statement, a retirement allowance shall consist of a(n)

   A. annuity plus a pension plus an actuarial equivalent
   B. annuity plus a pension plus reserve-for-increased-take-home-pay, if any
   C. annuity plus reserve-for-increased-take-home-pay, if any, plus final compensation
   D. pension plus reserve-for-increased-take-home-pay, if any, plus accumulated deductions

19.____

Question 20.

DIRECTIONS: Answer Question 20 SOLELY on the basis of the information in the paragraph below.

Membership in the retirement system shall cease upon the occurrence of any one of the following conditions: when the time out of service of any member who has total service of less than 25 years, shall aggregate more than 5 years; when the time out of service of any member who has total service of 25 years or more, shall aggregate more than 10 years; when any member shall have withdrawn more than 50% of his accumulated deductions; or when any member shall have withdrawn the cash benefit provided by Section B3-35.0 of the Administrative Code.

20. According to the information in the above paragraph, membership in the retirement system shall cease when an employee

   A. with 17 years of service has been on a leave of absence for 3 years
   B. withdraws 50% of his accumulated deductions
   C. with 28 years of service has been out of service for 10 years
   D. withdraws his cash benefits

20.____

KEY (CORRECT ANSWERS)

1. A
2. C
3. A
4. C
5. A

6. B
7. D
8. C
9. B
10. C

11. C
12. C
13. C
14. C
15. B

16. C
17. D
18. D
19. B
20. D

EXAMINATION SECTION
TEST 1

DIRECTIONS: Each question or incomplete statement is followed by several suggested answers or completions. Select the one that BEST answers the question or completes the statement. *PRINT THE LETTER OF THE CORRECT ANSWER IN THE SPACE AT THE RIGHT.*

NOTE: The following rules are to be used in solving the questions.

1. Each employee works until retirement.

2. An employee must work at least 5 years in order to be entitled to pension benefits, which are paid monthly.

3. Normal retirement is at age 65. The first monthly benefit for any eligible age will begin 1 month after retirement.

4. If an employee works beyond the age of 65, the pension amount will be increased by .3% for each additional month worked, up to a maximum of 18%. <u>Ex. 1</u>: An employee's pension at age 65 is $200 (per month). If the employee works until age 66, which is 12 additional months, the pension becomes $200 + (200)(.003)(12) = $207.20.

5. If an employee is at least 55 years old and has at least 10 years of service, he is eligible for an early retirement pension. In such an instance, the pension amount will be reduced by .5% for each month before the age of 65, up to a maximum of 60%. <u>Ex. 2</u>: An employee's pension at age 65 is $200. If the employee retires at age 63 (and assuming he has at least 10 years of service), the pension becomes $200 - (200)(.005)(24) = $176.00.

6. Unless otherwise indicated, the pension amounts are <u>gross</u> payments. An employee's pension will normally be subject to a 20% Federal tax, unless he chooses to deposit part or all of the gross amount into an IRA account. Any money deposited into an IRA is <u>not</u> taxed. The actual amount on the pension check is a <u>net</u> amount. <u>Ex. 3</u>: An employee's pension is $200. If he does not elect an IRA, his net amount becomes $200 - (.20)(200) or (200)(.80) = $160. Now suppose he had elected to deposit $50 into an IRA each month. Then, 200 - 50 = 150, and (150)(.80) = $120 = net amount. In this 2nd instance, the employee would actually have more disposable income ($120 + $50 = $170) than if he had not elected an IRA.

1. Consider the following employees:
   Ted is now 53 years 10 months old and was hired when he was 41 years old; Edna is now 55 years 6 months old and was hired when she was 48 years old; Chester is now 60 years old and was hired when he was 42 years old; Wendy is now 62 years old and was hired when she was 53 years old.
   Who can take early retirement immediately?

   A. Edna and Wendy
   B. Wendy *only*
   C. Chester and Wendy
   D. Chester *only*
   E. All four individuals

1.____

2. Which of the following are NOT eligible to receive a pension at age 65?

    I. Carmen is 60 years old and was hired when she was 58 years old.
    II. John is 63 years old and was hired when he was 61 years old.
    III. Stacy is 64 years old and was hired when she was 55 years old.

The CORRECT answer is:

  A. I only   B. II only   C. III only
  D. I, III   E. II, III

3. Richard is 58 years old and plans to retire at age 65. His gross monthly pension is $250, and he will put $100 into an IRA each month. What will be the net amount of his pension check?

  A. $200   B. $180   C. $150   D. $120   E. $100

4. Veronica is 61 years old and plans to retire at age 65. She was hired at age 55. Her gross monthly pension is $320, and she will put $230 into an IRA each month. What will be the net amount of her pension check?

  A. $72   B. $90   C. $122   D. $152   E. $184

5. Flora is 56 years old and plans to retire at age 65. Her gross monthly pension is $210, and the net amount of her pension check is $107.60.
How much of her pension is deposited into an IRA each month?

  A. $112.98   B. $102.40   C. $94.24   D. $86.08   E. $75.50

6. Jerry is eligible for a full pension of $340/month on 7/1/2007. If he elects to work until 1/31/2008 and does NOT elect an IRA, what will be the net amount of his pension check?

  A. $272.00   B. $277.71   C. $309.82   D. $341.93   E. $347.14

7. Nick is 62 years old and plans to retire at age 65. He was hired at age 50. If he puts $180 into an IRA each month and the net amount of his pension check is $179.68, what is the gross amount?

  A. $413.58   B. $404.60   C. $395.62   D. $341.65   E. $323.68

8. Noelle is eligible for a full pension of $520/month on 3/1/2007. If she works until 3/31/2008 and does NOT elect an IRA, what will be the net amount of her pension check?

  A. $416.00   B. $429.72   C. $432.22   D. $537.16   E. $540.28

9. Katie is eligible for a full pension of $600/month on 11/1/2007. She will NOT elect an IRA, but wants to work until she can get a net amount of $491.52 in her pension check. What is the earliest date in the year 2008 on which she can get this amount?

  A. Jan. 1   B. Feb. 1   C. Apr. 1   D. July 1   E. Oct. 1

10. Scott is eligible for a full pension of $850/month on 9/1/2007. He plans to work until 11/30/2009 and will put $160 into an IRA each month. What will be the net amount of his pension check?

  A. $607.08   B. $658.60   C. $710.60   D. $735.08   E. $758.85

11. Heather is eligible for a full pension of $910/month on 12/1/2007. She plans to work until 5/31/2009 and wants to put 30% of her increased pension amount into an IRA each month.
    What will be the net amount of her pension check?

    A. $518.78   B. $527.95   C. $537.12   D. $546.29   E. $555.46

11._____

12. Adam is eligible for a full pension on 5/1/2007. He has decided to work until 9/30/2007 and will put $250 into an IRA each month.
    If the net amount of his pension check will be $384.64, what will be the gross amount?

    A. $738.00   B. $730.80   C. $725.40   D. $720.00   E. $712.80

12._____

13. Rachel is 63 years 3 months old. Since she currently has only 6 months of service, she cannot retire at age 65 with a pension.
    If she decides to retire when she has 5 years of service, how old will she be?

    A. 65.5   B. 67.75   C. 68.25   D. 68.75   E. 70.5

13._____

14. Greg is 64 years 5 months old, with only 9 months of service. If he decides to retire when he has 6 years of service, how old will he be?

    A. 68 5/6   B. 69 2/3   C. 70 1/12   D. 70 5/12   E. 71 1/6

14._____

15. Lorraine is eligible for a full pension on 2/1/2007. She has decided to work until 3/31/2008 and will put $160 into an IRA each month.
    If the net amount of her pension check will be $324.23, what will be the gross amount?

    A. $419.30   B. $450.10   C. $480.90   D. $511.70   E. $542.50

15._____

16. Harriet is 52 years 4 months old as of 6/10/2007 and has over 10 years of service. On what date, in the year 2010, will she be eligible for an early retirement?

    A. June 1   B. Feb. 1   C. Mar. 1   D. Oct. 1   E. Nov. 1

16._____

17. Mike is eligible for a full pension of $950/month on 10/1/2008, but elects early retirement on 5/1/2007. Assuming a sufficient number of years of service, what will be the gross amount of his pension?

    A. $926.25   B. $901.55   C. $869.25   D. $837.55   E. $812.25

17._____

18. Theresa is eligible for a full pension of $755.50/month on 8/1/2010, but elects early retirement on 9/1/2006. Assuming a sufficient number of years of service, what will be the gross amount of her pension?

    A. $562.84   B. $566.62   C. $570.40   D. $574.14   E. $577.96

18._____

19. Beverly would have been eligible for a full pension of $1024/month, but will only get a gross amount of $860.16 due to early retirement. How many months before age 65 did she actually retire?

    A. 32   B. 30   C. 28   D. 26   E. 24

19._____

20. Andy would have been eligible for a full pension of $865.50 per month, but will only get a gross amount of $679.42 due to early retirement. How many months before age 65 did he actually retire?

    A. 41   B. 43   C. 45   D. 47   E. 49

20._____

21. Doreen has decided to retire 10 months before age 65. Assuming she will be eligible for early retirement and that her full pension would have been $680.40/month, if she does NOT elect an IRA, what will be the net amount of her pension check?   21._____

    A. $511.65   B. $517.10   C. $522.55   D. $528.00   E. $533.45

22. Eddie will retire 2 years 6 months before age 65. Assuming eligibility for early retirement and that his full pension would have been $1260/month, if he does NOT elect an IRA, what will be the net amount of his pension check?   22._____

    A. $796.32   B. $826.56   C. $856.80   D. $887.04   E. $917.28

23. Evelyn will retire 6 months before age 65. Assume she has eligibility for early retirement and that her full pension would have been $1075/month. If she will put $150 into an IRA each month, what will be the net amount of her pension check?   23._____

    A. $669.20   B. $684.20   C. $699.20   D. $714.20   E. $729.20

24. Isabel will retire 1 year before age 65. Assume she will be eligible for early retirement and that her full pension would have been $905/month. If the net amount of her pension is $632.56, how much is she putting into an IRA each month?   24._____

    A. $55   B. $60   C. $65   D. $70   E. $75

25. Ken is eligible for a full pension on 12/1/2007, but will receive a reduced pension as of 3/1/2007. He does NOT elect an IRA.   25._____
    If the net amount of his pension check is $859.96, what is the gross amount?

    A. $1205.60   B. $1185.60   C. $1165.60
    D. $1145.60   E. $1125.60

KEY (CORRECT ANSWERS)

1.	D	11.	C
2.	B	12.	D
3.	D	13.	B
4.	A	14.	B
5.	E	15.	E
6.	B	16.	C
7.	B	17.	C
8.	C	18.	E
9.	D	19.	A
10.	A	20.	B

21.	B
22.	C
23.	D
24.	B
25.	E

SOLUTIONS TO PROBLEMS

1. CORRECT ANSWER: D
   Only Chester satisfies the requirements of having BOTH the minimum 10 years of service and the minimum age of 55.

2. CORRECT ANSWER: B
   Only John will have fewer than 5 years of service when he is 65 years old.

3. CORRECT ANSWER: D
   250 - 100 = 150. Then, (150)(.80) = $120

4. CORRECT ANSWER: A
   320 - 230 = 90. Then, (90)(.80) = $72

5. CORRECT ANSWER: E
   Let x = amount put into an IRA. (210-x)(.80) = 107.60. Solving, x = $75.50

6. CORRECT ANSWER: B
   7 months past retirement age of 65 means a gross amount of 340 + (340)(7)(.003) = $347.14. Then, (347.14)(.80) = $277.71

7. CORRECT ANSWER: B
   Let x = gross amount. (x-180)(.80) = 179.68 Solving, x = $404.60

8. CORRECT ANSWER: C
   13 months past normal retirement means a gross amount of 520 + (520)(13)(.003) = $540.28. Then, (540.28)(.80) = $432.22

9. CORRECT ANSWER: D
   Let x = number of months. [600 + (100)(.003)(x)][.80] = 491.52. This simplifies to 480 + 1.44x = 491.52, so x = 8. Adding 8 months yields July 1, 2008.

10. CORRECT ANSWER: A
    850 + (850)(.003)(27) = 918.85. Then, 918.85 - 160 = 758.85. Finally, (758.85)(.80) = 607.08

11. CORRECT ANSWER: C
    910 + (910)(.003)(18) = 959.14. Then, 959.14 - (.30)(959.14) = 671.40. Finally, (671.40)(.80) = $537.12

12. CORRECT ANSWER: D
    Let x = gross amount. [x + (x)(5)(.003) - 250][.80] = 384.64 This simplifies to (1.5x - 250)(.80) = 384.64. Solving, x = $720.00

13. CORRECT ANSWER: B
    63 years 3 months + (5 years - 6 months) = 67 years 9 months = 67.75 years

14. CORRECT ANSWER: B
    64 years 5 months + (6 years - 9 months) = 69 years 8 months = 69 2/3 years

15. CORRECT ANSWER: E
    Let x = gross amount. [x + (x)(14)(.003) - 160][.80] = 324.23. This simplifies to (1.042x - 160)(.80) = 324.23. Then, 1.042x - 160 = 405.2875. Solving, x = $542.50

16. CORRECT ANSWER: C
    55 years - (52 years 4 months) = 2 years 8 months.
    Then, 6/10/2007 + 2 years 8 months rounds up to 3/1/2010

17. CORRECT ANSWER: C
    10/1/2008 - 5/1/2007 = 17 months. Then, 950 - (17)(.005)(950) = $869.25

18. CORRECT ANSWER: E
    8/1/2010 - 9/1/2006 = 47 months. Then, 755.50 - (47)(.005)(755.50) = $577.96

19. CORRECT ANSWER: A
    Let x = number of months. 1024 - (x)(.005)(1024) = 860.16 Solving, x = 32

20. CORRECT ANSWER: B
    Let x = number of months. 865.50 - (x)(.005)(865.50) = 679.42 Solving, x = 43

21. CORRECT ANSWER: B
    680.40 - (10)(.005)(680.40) = 646.38. Thus, (646.38)(.80) = $517.10

22. CORRECT ANSWER: C
    1260 - (30)(.005)(1260) = 1071, and (1071)(.80) = $856.80

23. CORRECT ANSWER: D
    1075 - (6)(.005)(1075) = 1042.75. Then, 1042.75 - 150 = 892.75 Finally, (892.75)(.80) = $714.20

24. CORRECT ANSWER: B
    Let x = amount put into an IRA each month. 905 - (12)(905)(.005)= 850.70. Then, (850.70 - x)(.80) = 632.56. This simplifies to 680.56 - .80x = 632.56. Solving, x = $60

25. CORRECT ANSWER: E
    Let x = gross amount. [x - (9)(.005)(x)][.80] = 859.96 This simplifies to .764x = 859.96, so x = $1125.60

TEST 2

DIRECTIONS: Each question or incomplete statement is followed by several suggested answers or completions. Select the one that BEST answers the question or completes the statement. *PRINT THE LETTER OF THE CORRECT ANSWER IN THE SPACE AT THE RIGHT.*

1. Irene is eligible for a full pension on 2/1/2011, but will receive a reduced pension as of 12/1/2006. She has elected to put $200 into an IRA each month. If the net amount of her pension is $365.48, what would be the gross amount of her full pension?

    A. $815.80   B. $845.80   C. $875.80   D. $905.80   E. $935.80

1.____

Questions 2-25.

DIRECTIONS: In answering Questions 2 through 25, assume these are newly hired employees. Their gross pensions (monthly) are calculated using the following chart.

YEARS OF SERVICE UPON RETIRING

PAYMENT OPTION	At Least 5 Years But Less Than 10 Years	At Least 10 Years But Less Than 20 Years	At Least 20 Years But Less Than 30 Years	At Least 30 Years
Plan 1 - Payable For Life Only	*EM = $180 SP = N/A	EM = $250 SP = N/A	EM = $340 SP = N/A	EM = $450 SP = N/A
Plan 2 - Payable For Life With 10 Years Guaranteed	EM = $160 SP = $160 (if appl.)	EM = $225 SP = $225 (if appl.)	EM = $310 SP = $310 (if appl.)	EM = $415 SP = $415 (if appl.)
Plan 3 - 50% Joint and Survivor	EM = $140 SP = $70	EM - $200 SP = $100	EM = $280 SP = $140	EM = $380 SP = $190
Plan 4 - 100% Joint and Survivor	EM = $120 SP = $120	EM = $170 SP = $170	EM = $235 SP = $235	EM = $315 SP = $315

*For this chart, EM = Employee, SP = Spouse. Each amount listed is the gross amount per month. Assume the spouse is always the beneficiary.

<u>EXPLANATION OF TERMS FROM THE CHART</u>

<u>Payable For Life Only</u>
    The benefit is payable only to the employee until he dies. There is no beneficiary.
<u>Ex. 1</u>: An employee lives 7 months after retiring. If he has 6 years of service when he retires, his gross pension will total ($180)(7) = $1260.

Payable For Life With 10 Years Guaranteed

The benefit will be payable to the employee for the longer of the time he lives beyond retirement or 10 years. If the employee dies within 10 years, the same benefit will be paid to the beneficiary until 10 years worth of benefits has been paid. Ex. 2: An employee lives 12 years after retiring and has 12 years of service. His total gross pension = ($225)(12) = $2700. Nothing will be paid to the beneficiary. Ex. 3: An employee lives 8 years after retiring with 12 years of service. Then, his gross pension = ($225)(8) = $1800, plus ($225)(2) = $450 will be paid to the beneficiary. The total amount of the gross pension = 1800 + 450 = $2250.

50% Joint and Survivor

A specific benefit is paid to the employee upon retiring. When he dies, half that benefit is paid to the beneficiary until the beneficiary dies. Ex. 4: An employee with 5 years of service dies 3 months after retiring. The surviving beneficiary (which is the spouse in ALL problems) lives 5 months after the death of the employee. The total amount of the gross pension = ($140)(3) + ($70)(5) = $770.

100% Joint and Survivor

A specific benefit is paid to the employee upon retiring. When he dies, the same benefit is paid to the beneficiary until the beneficiary dies. Ex. 5: An employee with 25 years of service dies 4 months after retiring. The surviving beneficiary (spouse) lives 2 months after the death of the employee. The total amount of the gross pension = ($235)(4) + ($235)(2) = $1410.

2. Maxine is 57 years old and plans to retire at age 65. If she chooses Plan 1 and lives until she is 71 years old, what will be the total amount of her gross pension?

   A. $13,440 B. $12,960 C. $12,480 D. $12,000 E. $11,520

3. Ginger is 53 years old and plans to retire at age 65. If she chooses Plan 2 and lives until she is 69 years 6 months old, what will be the total amount of her gross pension?

   A. $12,150 B. $19,200 C. $22,000 D. $24,500 E. $27,000

4. Larry is 37 years old and plans to retire at age 65. If he chooses Plan 2 and lives until he is 78 years old, what will be the total amount of his gross pension?

   A. $37,200 B. $42,780 C. $48,360 D. $56,550 E. $64,740

5. Aaron is 50 years old and plans to retire at age 65. If he chooses Plan 3, lives until he is 68 years 4 months old, and his wife lives 2 years beyond his death, what will be the total amount of his gross pension?

   A. $10,400 B. $11,200 C. $12,000 D. $12,800 E. $13,600

6. Juanita is 32 years old and plans to retire at age 65. Suppose she chooses Plan 4, lives until she is 74 years old, and her husband lives 3 years, 5 months beyond her death. What will be the total amount of her gross pension?

   A. $35,015 B. $40,975 C. $46,935 D. $52,895 E. $58,855

7. Jennifer is 25 years old and plans to retire at age 65. She is undecided about whether to choose Plan 1 or Plan 2. If she lives until she is 76 years 8 months old, how much more will be the total gross pension with Plan 1?

   A. $4200 B. $4400 C. $4700 D. $4900 E. $5100

8. Amanda is 41 years old and plans to retire at age 65. Suppose she chooses Plan 3 and lives until she is 69 years old.
   If the total amount of her gross pension is to exceed $16,200, what is the minimum number of months her husband must live beyond her death?

   A. 17   B. 18   C. 19   D. 20   E. 21

   8._____

9. Dennis is 58 years old and plans to retire at age 65. Suppose he chooses Plan 4 and lives until the age of 73 years 3 months.
   If the total amount of his gross pension is to exceed $13,600, what is the minimum number of months his wife must live beyond his death?

   A. 14   B. 15   C. 16   D. 17   E. 18

   9._____

10. Lester is 48 years old and plans to retire at age 65. He is undecided about whether to choose Plan 1 or Plan 2.
    If he lives until he is 73 years 6 months old, how much more will be the total gross pension with Plan 2?

    A. $1900   B. $1800   C. $1700   D. $1600   E. $1500

    10._____

11. Kathleen is 38 years old and plans to retire at age 65. If she chooses Plan 1 and lives until she is 75 years 6 months old, what will be the total amount of her net pension assuming she does NOT elect an IRA?

    A. $31,500   B. $34,272   C. $37,044   D. $39,942   E. $42,840

    11._____

12. Charlene is 23 years old and plans to retire at age 65. If she chooses Plan 3, lives to the age of 67 years 3 months, and her husband lives 1 year beyond her death, what will be the total amount of her net pension, assuming she does NOT elect an IRA?

    A. $10,032   B. $10,659   C. $11,286   D. $11,914   E. $12,540

    12._____

13. Victor is 44 years old and plans to retire at age 67. If he elects Plan 2 and lives until the age of 71 years 4 months, what will be the total amount of his gross pension?

    A. $15,540   B. $16,120   C. $16,700   D. $17,280   E. $17,860

    13._____

14. Zeke is 24 years old and will retire at age 69.
    If he chooses Plan 1, what is the minimum number of months he must live past age 69 for his total gross pension to exceed $9260?

    A. 14   B. 15   C. 16   D. 17   E. 18

    14._____

15. Tanya is 54 years old and will retire at age 68.
    If she chooses Plan 4, lives until the age of 69 years 6 months, and her husband lives 2 years beyond her death, what is the total amount of her gross pension?

    A. $8160   B. $7910   C. $7660   D. $7410   E. $7160

    15._____

16. Lori is 50 years old and will retire at age 66.
    If she chooses Plan 2 and lives until the age of 67 years 3 months, what is the minimum number of months her beneficiary must live past her death for the total gross pension to exceed $6000?

    A. 6   B. 11   C. 16   D. 21   E. 26

    16._____

17. Eileen is 44 years old and will retire at age 60.
    If she chooses Plan 2 and lives to the age of 68, what will be the total amount of her gross pension?

    A. $18,900 B. $17,955 C. $17,010 D. $16,065 E. $15,120

18. George is 35 years old and will retire at the age of 61 years 6 months. Suppose he chooses Plan 3 and lives to age 66.
    If his wife lives 1 year 6 months beyond his death, what will be the total amount of his gross pension?

    A. $7484.60   B. $9122.40   C. $10,760.40
    D. $12,297.60   E. $13,935.60

19. Judith is 26 years old and will retire at age 58. Suppose she chooses Plan 4 and lives to age 62.
    What is the minimum number of months her husband must live beyond Judith's death if the gross pension is to exceed $10,500?

    A. 9 B. 10 C. 11 D. 12 E. 13

20. Luanne is 39 years old and will retire at the age of 63 years 8 months. Suppose she chooses Plan 1 and lives to the age of 70.
    If she does NOT elect an IRA, what will be the total amount of her net pension?

    A. $19,018.24   B. $20,206.88   C. $21,395.52
    D. $22,584.16   E. $23,772.80

21. Pierre is 31 years old and will retire at age 62. Suppose he chooses Plan 3, lives to age 66, and his wife lives 1 year 4 months past his death.
    If $100 is put into an IRA each month after he retires, what will be the total amount of his net pension check?

    A. $8125.44   B. $8363.52   C. $8601.60
    D. $8839.68   E. $9077.76

22. Bruce is 58 years old and will retire at age 64. Suppose he chooses Plan 4, lives to the age of 67 years 6 months, and his wife lives 9 years past his death.
    If $40 is put into an IRA each month after he retires, what will be the total amount of the net pension checks?

    A. $2562.24   B. $2766.24   C. $2970.24
    D. $3174.24   E. $3378.24

23. Sharon is 43 years old and will retire at age 65. Suppose she chooses Plan 3, lives to the age of 68 years 6 months, and her husband lives 10 months past her death. If $70 is put into an IRA each month after she retires until her death and $50 is put into an IRA following her death until her husband dies, what will be the total amount of the net pension checks?

    A. $7888 B. $7608 C. $7328 D. $7048 E. $6768

24. Celeste is 59 years old and will retire at age 65. Suppose she chooses Plan 2 and lives to the age of 78. At retirement, $25 is put into an IRA each month for 5 years.
    How much money is put into an IRA for each month for the next 8 years if the total amount of the net pension checks is $16,310.40?

    A. $32 B. $34 C. $36 D. $38 E. $40

25. Ernie is 39 years old and will retire at age 63. Suppose he chooses Plan 4, lives to the age of 64 years 6 months, and his wife lives 8 months past his death. At retirement, $45 is deposited into an IRA for the rest of Ernie's life.
How much money needs to be put into an IRA for the next 8 months if the total amount of the net pension checks is $3487.04?

   A. $20   B. $22   C. $24   D. $26   E. $28

25.____

KEY (CORRECT ANSWERS)

1.	C	11.	B
2.	B	12.	A
3.	E	13.	D
4.	C	14.	E
5.	A	15.	B
6.	C	16.	B
7.	D	17.	A
8.	D	18.	E
9.	B	19.	B
10.	E	20.	A

21. D
22. C
23. E
24. A
25. D

6 (#2)

SOLUTIONS TO PROBLEMS

1. CORRECT ANSWER: C
   2/1/2011 - 12/1/2006 = 50 months. Let x = gross amount. [x - (50)(.005)(x) - 200][.80] = 365.48. This simplifies to .6x - 160 = 365.48. Solving, x = $875.80

2. CORRECT ANSWER: B
   (180)(12)(6) = $12,960

3. CORRECT ANSWER: E
   (225)(12)(10) = $27,000. Note: Although she only lives 4 years 6 months beyond age 65, Plan 2 allows for payments for a full 10 years.

4. CORRECT ANSWER: C
   (310)(12)(13) = $48,360

5. CORRECT ANSWER: A
   (200)(12)(3 1/3) = 8000. Then, 8000 + (100)(24) = $10,400

6. CORRECT ANSWER: C
   (315)(12)(9) = 34,020. Then, 34,020 + (315)(41) = $46,935

7. CORRECT ANSWER: D
   (450)(140) - (415)(140) = $4900

8. CORRECT ANSWER: D
   Let x = number of months. (280)(48) + (x)(140) > 16,200. This reduces to 140x > 2760. Solving, x > 19.7 (approx.) Thus, 20 is the lowest value of x.

9. CORRECT ANSWER: B
   Let x = number of months. (120)(99) + (x)(120) > 13,600. Then, x > 14 1/3, so 15 is the lowest value of x.

10. CORRECT ANSWER: E
    (225)(12)(10) - (250)(12)(8 1/2) = $1500

11. CORRECT ANSWER: B
    (340)(12)(10 1/2)(.80) = $34,272

12. CORRECT ANSWER: A
    (380)(27) + (190)(12) = 12,540. Then, (12,540)(.80) = $10,032

13. CORRECT ANSWER: D
    310 + (310)(.003)(24) = 332.32. Since 71 years 4 months -67 years = 52 months, we get the gross amount of (332.3252) * $17.280

14. CORRECT ANSWER: E
    450 + (450) (.003)(48) = 514.80. Let x = number of months. Then, 514.80x > 9260, so x > 17.988. Thus, 18 months are needed.

15. CORRECT ANSWER: B
    170 + (170)(.003)(36) = 188.36. Then, (188.36)(18+24) = 7911.12 = $7910

16. CORRECT ANSWER: B
    225 + (225)(.003)(12) = 233.10. Let x = number of months. Then, (233.10)(15) + 233.10x > 6000. Finally, x > 10.74, so 11 months are needed.

17. CORRECT ANSWER: A
    225 - (225)(.005)(60) = $157.50. Since 10 years of payments are guaranteed, (157.50)(120) = $18,900

18. CORRECT ANSWER: E
    280 - (280)(.005)(42) = 221.20. Recognizing the wife gets $110.60/month, (221.20)(54) + (110.60)(18) = $13,935.60

19. CORRECT ANSWER: B
    315 - (315)(.005)(84) = 182.70. Let x = number of months needed. Then, (182.70)(48) + (182.70)(x) > 10,500. Solving, x > 9.47, so 10 months are needed.

20. CORRECT ANSWER: A
    340 - (340)(.005)(16) = 312.80/month. Then, we get (312.80)(.80)(76) = $19,018.24

21. CORRECT ANSWER: D
    380 - (380)(.005)(36) = 311.60/month and the wife gets 155.80/month (these are gross amounts). Now, 311.60 - 100.00 = 211.60, and (211.60)(.80)(48) = 8125.44. Likewise, 155.80 - 100.00 = 55.80, and (55.80)(.80)(16) = 714.24. Finally, 8125.44 + 714.24 = 8839.68

22. CORRECT ANSWER: C
    120 - (120)(.005)(12) = 112.80/month. 112.80 - 40 = 72.80, and (72.80)(.80) = 58.24. Finally, (58.24)(42) + (58.24)(9) = $2970.24

23. CORRECT ANSWER: E
    280 - 70 = 210. Then, (210)(.80)(36 months) = 6048. The husband gets a gross amount of $140/month. 140 - 50 = 90. Then, (90)(.80)(10 months) = 720. Finally, 6048 + 720 = $6768

24. CORRECT ANSWER: A
    160 - 25 = 135. Then, (135)(.80)(60 months) = 6480. Let x = amount deposited each month for the next 8 years. (160 - x)(.80)(96 months) = 12,288 - 76.8x. Then, 6480 + 12,288 - 76.8x = 16,310.40. Solving, x = $32

25. CORRECT ANSWER: D
    235 - (235)(.005)(24) = 206.80. Then, 206.80 - 45 = 161.80. (161.80)(.80)(18 months) = 2329.92. Let x = amount deposited each month for the next 8 months. (206.80 - x)(.80)(8 months) = 1323.52 - 6.4x. Then, 2329.92 + 1323.52 - 6.4x = 3487.04. Solving, x = $26

EFFECTIVELY INTERACTING WITH AGENCY STAFF AND MEMBERS OF THE PUBLIC

Test material will be presented in a multiple-choice question format.

Test Task: You will be presented with a variety of situations in which you must apply knowledge of how best to interact with other people.

SAMPLE QUESTION:

A person approaches you expressing anger about a recent action by your department.
Which one of the following should be your first response to this person?
- A. Interrupt to say you cannot discuss the situation until he calms down.
- B. Say you are sorry that he has been negatively affected by your department's action.
- C. Listen and express understanding that he has been upset by your department's action.
- D. Give him an explanation of the reasons for your department's action.

The CORRECT answer to this sample question is Choice C.
Solution:

Choice A is not correct. It would be inappropriate to interrupt. In addition, saying that you cannot discuss the situation until the person calms down will likely aggravate the person further.

Choice B is not correct. Apologizing for your department's action implies that the action was improper.

Choice C is the correct answer to this question. By listening and expressing understanding that your department's action has upset the person, you demonstrate that you have heard and understand the person's feelings and point of view.

Choice D is not correct. While an explanation of the reasons for the action may be appropriate at a later time, at this moment the person is angry and would not be receptive to such an explanation.

EXAMINATION SECTION

TEST 1

DIRECTIONS: Each question or incomplete statement is followed by several suggested answers or completions. Select the one that BEST answers the question or completes the statement. *PRINT THE LETTER OF THE CORRECT ANSWER IN THE SPACE AT THE RIGHT.*

1. Good procedure in handling complaints from the public may be divided into the following four principal stages:
    I. Investigation of the complaint
    II. Receipt of the complaint
    III. Assignment of responsibility for investigation and correction
    IV. Notification of correction

    The ORDER in which these stages ordinarily come is:
    A. III, II, I, IV   B. II, III, I, IV   C. II, III, IV, I   D. II, IV, III, I

    1._____

2. The department may expect the MOST severe public criticism if
    A. it asks for an increase in its annual budget
    B. it purchases new and costly street cleaning equipment
    C. sanitation officers and men are reclassified to higher salary grades
    D. there is delay in cleaning streets of snow

    2._____

3. The MOST important function of public relations in the department should be to
    A. develop cooperation on the part of the public in keeping streets clean
    B. get stricter penalties enacted for health code violations
    C. recruit candidates for entrance positions who ca be developed into supervisors
    D. train career personnel so that they can advance in the department

    3._____

4. The one of the following which has MOST frequently elicited unfavorable public comment has been
    A. dirty sidewalks or streets   B. dumping on lot
    C. failure to curb dogs   D. overflowing garbage cans

    4._____

5. It has been suggested that, as a public relations measure, sections hold *open house* for the public.
    The MOST effective time for this would be
    A. during the summer when children are not in school and can accompany their parents
    B. during the winter when show is likely to fall and the public can see snow removal preparations
    C. immediately after a heavy snow storm when department snow removal operations are in full progress
    D. when street sanitation is receiving general attention as during *Keep City Clean* week

    5._____

25

6. When a public agency conducts a public relations program, it is MOST likely to find that each recipient of its message will
   A. disagree with the basic purpose of the message if the officials are not well known to him
   B. accept the message if it is presented by someone perceived as having a definite intention to persuade
   C. ignore the message unless it is presented in a literate and clever manner
   D. give greater attention to certain portions of the message as a result of his individual and cultural differences

7. Following are three statements about public relations and communications:
   I. A person who seeks to influence public opinion can speed up a trend
   II. Mass communications is the exposure of a mass audience to an idea
   III. All media are equally effective in reaching opinion leaders
   Which of the following choices CORRECTLY classifies the above statements into those which are correct and those which are not?
   A. I and II are correct, but III is not.
   B. II and III are correct, but I is not.
   C. I and III are correct, but II is not.
   D. III is correct, but I and II are not.

8. Public relations experts say that MAXIMUM effect for a message results from
   A. concentrating in one medium
   B. ignoring mass media and concentrating on *opinion makers*
   C. presenting only those factors which support a given position
   D. using a combination of two or more of the available media

9. To assure credibility and avoid hostility, the public relations man MUST
   A. make certain his message is truthful, not evasive or exaggerated
   B. make sure his message contains some dire consequence if ignored
   C. repeat the message often enough so that it cannot be ignored
   D. try to reach as many people and groups as possible

10. The public relations man MUST be prepared to assume that members of his audience
    A. may have developed attitudes toward his proposals—favorable, neutral, or unfavorable
    B. will be immediately hostile
    C. will consider his proposals with an open mind
    D. will invariably need an introduction to his subject

11. The one of the following statements that is CORRECT is:
    A. When a stupid question is asked of you by the public, it should be disregarded
    B. If you insist on formality between you and the public, the public will not be able to ask stupid questions that cannot be answered
    C. The public should be treated courteously, regardless of how stupid their questions may be
    D. You should explain to the public how stupid their questions are

12. With regard to public relations, the MOST important item which should be emphasized in an employee training program is that
    A. each inspector is a public relations agent
    B. an inspector should give the public all the information it asks for
    C. it is better to make mistakes and give erroneous information than to tell the public that you do not know the correct answer to their problem
    D. public relations is so specialized a field that only persons specially trained in it should consider it

12._____

13. Members of the public frequently ask about departmental procedures. Of the following, it is BEST to
    A. advise the public to put the question in writing so that he can get a proper formal reply
    B. refuse to answer because this is a confidential matter
    C. explain the procedure as briefly as possible
    D. attempt to avoid the issue by discussing other matters

13._____

14. The effectiveness of a public relations program in a public agency such as the authority is BEST indicated by the
    A. amount of mass media publicity favorable to the policies of the authority
    B. morale of those employees who directly serve the patrons of the authority
    C. public's understanding and support of the authority's program and policies
    D. number of complaint received by the authority from patrons using its facilities

14._____

15. In an attempt to improve public opinion about a certain idea, the BEST course of action for an agency to take would be to present the
    A. clearest statements of the idea even though the language is somewhat technical
    B. idea as the result of long-term studies
    C. idea in association with something familiar to most people
    D. idea as the viewpoint of the majority leaders

15._____

16. The fundamental factor in any agency's community relations program is
    A. an outline of the objectives
    B. relations with the media
    C. the everyday actions of the employees
    D. a well-planned supervisory program

16._____

17. The FUNDAMENTAL factor in the success of a community relations program is
    A. true commitment by the community
    B. true commitment by the administration
    C. a well-planned, systematic approach
    D. the actions of individuals in their contacts with the public

17._____

18. The statement below which is LEAST correct is:
    A. Because of selection standards, the supervisor frequently encounters problems resulting from subordinates' inability to express themselves in the language of the profession.
    B. Distortion of the meaning of a communication is usually brought about by a failure to use language that has a precise meaning to others.
    C. The term *filtering* is the distortion or dilution of content of a communication that occurs as information is passed from individual to individual.
    D. The complexity of the *communications net* will directly affect.

19. Consider the following three statements that may or may not be CORRECT:
    I. In order to prevent the stifling of communications flow, supervisors should insist that employees use the formal communications network.
    II. Two-way communications are faster and more accurate than one-way communications.
    III. There is a direct correlation between the effectiveness of communications and the total setting in which they occur.
    The choice below which MOST accurately describes the above statement is:
    A. All three are correct.
    B. All three are incorrect.
    C. More than one statement is correct.
    D. Only one of the statements is correct.

20. The statement below which is MOST inaccurate is:
    A. The supervisor's most important tool in learning whether or not he is communicating well is feedback.
    B. Follow-up is essential if useful feedback is to be obtained.
    C. Subordinates are entitled, as a matter of right, to explanations from management concerning the reasons for orders or directives.
    D. A skilled supervisor is often able to use the grapevine to good advantage.

21. *Since concurrence by those affected is not sought, this kind of communication can be issued with relative ease.*
    The kind of communication being referred to in this quotation is
    A. autocratic   B. democratic   C. directive   D. free-rein

22. The statement below which is LEAST correct is:
    A. Clarity is more important in oral communicating than in written since the readers of a written communication can read it over again.
    B. Excessive use of abbreviations in written communications should be avoided.
    C. Short sentences with simple words are preferred over complex sentences and difficult words in a written communication.
    D. The *newspaper* style of writing ordinarily simplifies expression and facilitates understanding.

23. Which one of the following is the MOST important factor for the department to consider in building a good public image?
    A. A good working relationship with the news media
    B. An efficient community relations program
    C. An efficient system for handling citizen complaints
    D. The proper maintenance of facilities and equipment
    E. The behavior of individuals in their contacts with the public.

24. It has been said that the ability to communicate clearly and concisely is the MOST important single skill of the supervisor.
    Consider the following statements:
    I. The adage, *Actions speak louder than words*, has NO application in superior/subordinate communications since good communications are accomplished with words.
    II. The environment in which a communication takes place will *rarely* determine its effect.
    III. Words are symbolic representations which must be associated with past experience or else they are meaningless.
    The choice below which MOST accurately describes the above statements is:
    A. I, II, and III are correct.
    B. I and II are correct, but III is not.
    C. I and III are correct, but II is not.
    D. III is correct, but I and II are not.
    E. I, II, and III are incorrect.

25. According to expert opinion, the effectiveness of an organization is very dependent upon good upward, downward, and lateral communications. Lateral communications are most important to the activity of coordinating the efforts of organizational units. Before real communication can take place at any level, barriers to communication must be recognized, understood, and removed.
    Consider the following three statements:
    I. The *principal* barrier to good communications is a failure to establish empathy between sender and receiver.
    II. The difference in status or rank between the sender and receiver of a communication may be a communications barrier.
    III. Communications are easier if they travel upward from subordinate to superior
    The choice below which MOST accurately describes the above statements is:
    A. I, II and III are incorrect.   B. I and II are incorrect.
    C. I, II, and III are correct.   D. I and II are correct.
    E. I and III are incorrect.

KEY (CORRECT ANSWERS)

1.	B		11.	C
2.	D		12.	A
3.	A		13.	C
4.	A		14.	C
5.	D		15.	C
6.	D		16.	C
7.	A		17.	D
8.	D		18.	A
9.	A		19.	D
10.	A		20.	C

21. A
22. A
23. E
24. D
25. E

EXAMINATION SECTION
TEST 1

DIRECTIONS: Each question or incomplete statement is followed by several suggested answers or completions. Select the one that BEST answers the question or completes the statement. *PRINT THE LETTER OF THE CORRECT ANSWER IN THE SPACE AT THE RIGHT.*

1. Companies with successful customer service organizations usually experience each of the following EXCEPT
    A. fewer customer complaints
    B. greater response to advertising
    C. lower marketing costs
    D. more repeat business

    1.____

2. To be most useful to an organization, feedback received from customers should be each of the following EXCEPT
    A. centered on internal customers
    B. orgoing
    C. focused on a limited number of indicators
    D. available to every employee in the organization

    2.____

3. Instead of directly saying *no* to a customer, service representatives will usually get BEST results with a reply that begins with the words:
    A. I'll try
    B. I don't believe
    C. You can
    D. It's not our policy

    3.____

4. Once a customer problem is identified, each of the following should become a part of the service recovery process EXCEPT
    A. following up on the problem resolution
    B. making whatever promises are necessary
    C. providing the customer with what was originally requested
    D. listening and responding to every complaint given by the customer

    4.____

5. The percentage of an organization's annual business that involves repeat customers is CLOSEST to
    A. 25%
    B. 45%
    C. 65%
    D. 85%

    5.____

6. Of the following, the _____ is NOT generally considered to be a major source of *service promise*.
    A. customer service representative
    B. organization
    C. particular department that delivers product to the customer
    D. customer

    6.____

7. A customer appears to be mildly irritated when lodging a complaint. The MOST appropriate action for a service representative to take while attempting resolution is to
   A. allow venting of frustrations
   B. enlist the customer in generating solutions
   C. show emotional neutrality
   D. create calm

8. If an organization loses one customer who normally spends $50 per week, the projected result of reduction in sales for the following year will be APPROXIMATELY
   A. $2,600   B. $12,400   C. $124,000   D. $950,000

9. The majority of *service promises* originate from
   A. organizational management
   B. customer service professionals
   C. the customers' expectations
   D. organizational marketing

10. To arrive at a *fair fix* to a service problem, one should FIRSTS
    A. offer an apology for the problem
    B. ask probing questions to understand and confirm the nature of the problem
    C. listen to the customer's description of the problem
    D. determine and implement a solution to the problem

11. Which of the following is NOT generally considered to be a function of *open questioning* when dealing with a customer?
    A. Defining problems
    B. Confirming an order
    C. Getting more information
    D. Establishing customer needs

12. When dealing with a customer, service representatives should generally use the pronoun
    A. *they*, meaning the company as a whole
    B. *they*, meaning the department to whom the complaint will be referred
    C. *I*, meaning themselves, as representatives of the organization
    D. *we*, meaning themselves and the customer

13. A customer service representative demonstrates product and service knowledge by
    A. anticipating the changing needs of customers
    B. soliciting feedback from customers about customer service
    C. studying the capabilities of the office computer system
    D. knowing what questions are asked most by customers about a product or service

14. When listening to a customer during a face-to-face meeting, the MOST appropriate non-verbal gesture is
    A. clenched fists
    B. leaning slightly toward a customer
    C. hands casually in pockets
    D. standing with crossed arms

15. Before breaking or bending an existing service rule in order to better serve a customer, a representative should be aware of each of the following EXCEPT the
    A. reason for the rule
    B. location of a written copy of the rule and policy
    C. consequences of not following the rule
    D. situations in which the rule is applicable

16. The LEAST likely reason for a dissatisfied customer's failure to complain about a product or service is that the customer
    A. does not think the complaint will produce the desired results
    B. is unaware of the proper channels through which to voice his/her complaint
    C. does not believe he/she has the time to spend on the complaint
    D. does not believe anyone in the organization really cares about the complaint

17. Most research shows that _____% of what is communicated between people during face-to-face meetings is conveyed through entirely nonverbal cues.
    A. 10   B. 30   C. 50   D. 80

18. When a customer submits a written complaint, the representative should write a response that avoids
    A. addressing every single component of the customer's complaint
    B. a personal tone
    C. the use of a pre-formulated response structure
    D. mentioning future business transactions

19. A customer service representative spends several hours practicing with the various forms and paperwork required by the company for handling customer service situations.
    Which of the following basic areas of learning is the representative trying to improve upon?
    A. Interpersonal skills
    B. Product and service knowledge
    C. Customer knowledge
    D. Technical skills

20. If a customer service representative must deal with other members of a service team in order to resolve a problem, the representative should avoid
    A. developing personal relationships
    B. giving others credit for ideas that clearly were not theirs
    C. circumventing uncooperative team members by quietly contacting a superior
    D. involving customers in the resolution of a complaint

21. A customer service representative is willing to help customers promptly.
    Which of the following service factors is the representative able to demonstrate?
    A. Assurance
    B. Responsiveness
    C. Empathy
    D. Reliability

22. A service representative begins work in a specialized order entry job and son learns that many customers call in with orders at the last minute, causing her routine to be thrown out of balance and creating stress.
After studying the ordering patterns of all clients, the MOST effective resolution to the problem would be to
   A. mail reminder notices to habitually late customers in advance of typical ordering dates to establish lead time
   B. telephone habitually late customers a few days before their typical ordering dates to establish lead time
   C. place the orders of habitually late customers in advance, changing them later if necessary
   D. establish and enforce a rigid lead-time deadline to create more manageable client behavior

23. For BEST results, customer service representatives will improve service by considering themselves to be representative of
   A. the entire organization
   B. the department receiving the complaint
   C. the customer
   D. an adversary of the organization, who will fight along with the customer

24. Of all the customers who stop doing business with organizations, ____% do so because of product dissatisfaction.
   A. 15   B. 40   C. 65   D. 80

25. When using the *problem-solving* approach to solve the problem of a dissatisfied customer, the LAST step should be to
   A. double check for customer satisfaction
   B. identify the customer's expectations
   C. outline a solution or alternatives
   D. take action on the problem

KEY (CORRECT ANSWERS)

1.	B		11.	B
2.	A		12.	C
3.	C		13.	D
4.	B		14.	B
5.	C		15.	B
6.	C		16.	C
7.	B		17.	C
8.	A		18.	C
9.	B		19.	D
10.	C		20.	C

21. B
22. B
23. A
24. A
25. A

TEST 2

DIRECTIONS: Each question or incomplete statement is followed by several suggested answers or completions. Select the one that BEST answers the question or completes the statement. *PRINT THE LETTER OF THE CORRECT ANSWER IN THE SPACE AT THE RIGHT.*

1. Of the following, the LEAST likely reason for a customer to telephone an organization or department is to
   A. voice an objection
   B. make a statement
   C. offer praise
   D. ask a question

   1.____

2. Customer service usually requires each of the following EXCEPT
   A. product knowledge
   B. friendliness and approachability
   C. problem-solving skills
   D. company/organization knowledge

   2.____

3. According to research, a typical dissatisfied customer will tell about _____ people how dissatisfied he/she is with an organization's product or service.
   A. 3
   B. 5
   C. 10
   D. 20

   3.____

4. When a service target is provided by manager, it is MOST important for a service representative to know the
   A. nature of the customer database associated with the target
   B. formula for achieving the target
   C. methods used by other service personnel for achieving the target
   D. purpose behind the target

   4.____

5. Typically, customers cause about _____ of the service and product problems they complain about.
   A. 1/5
   B. 1/3
   C. 1/2
   D. 2/3

   5.____

6. When a dissatisfied customer complains to a service representative, making a sale is NOT considered to be good service when the
   A. customer appreciates being changed to a different service or product
   B. the original product or service is in need of additional parts or components to be complete
   C. the customer remains angry about the original complaint
   D. the original product or service is in need of repair

   6.____

7. As service representatives, personnel would be LEAST likely to be responsible for
   A. service
   B. marketing
   C. problem-solving
   D. sales

   7.____

8. When writing a memorandum on a customer complaint, _____ can be considered optional by a service representative.
   A. the date the complaint was filed and/or the problem occurred
   B. a summary of the customer's comments
   C. the address of the customer
   D. a suggestion for correcting the situation

   8.____

9. In most successful organizations, customer service is considered PRIMARILY to be the domain of the
    A. entire organization
    B. sales department
    C. complaint department
    D. service department

10. According to MOST research, the cost of attracting a new customer, in relation to the cost of retaining a current customer, is about
    A. half as much
    B. about the same
    C. twice as much
    D. five times as much

11. If a customer service representative is unable to do what a customer asks, the representative should avoid
    A. quoting organizational policy regarding the customer's request
    B. explaining why it cannot be done
    C. making specific statements
    D. offering alternatives

12. When a customer presents a service representative with a request, the representative's FIRST reaction should usually be a(n)
    A. apology
    B. friendly greeting
    C. statement of organizational policy regarding the request
    D. request for clarifying information

13. It is NOT a primary reason for written communication with customers to
    A. create documentation
    B. solidify relationships
    C. confirm understanding
    D. solicit business contact

14. Of the following, which would be LEAST frustrating for a customer to hear from a service representative?
    A. You will have to
    B. I will do my best
    C. Let me see what I can do
    D. He/she should be back any minute

15. A customer appears to be mildly irritated when lodging a complaint. It is MOST appropriate for a service representative to demonstrate _____ in reaction to the complaint.
    A. urgency
    B. empathy
    C. nonchalance
    D. surprise

16. The _____ would be indirectly served by an individual who takes customer orders at an organization's telephone center.
    A. customer
    B. management personnel
    C. billing agents
    D. warehouse staff

17. Based on the actions of a customer service representative, customers will be MOST likely to make judgments concerning each of the following EXCEPT the
    A. kind of people employed by the organization
    B. company's value system
    C. organization's commitment to advertised promises
    D. value of the organization's product

18. When dealing with customers, a service representative's apologies, if necessary, should NOT be
    A. immediate   B. official   C. sincere   D. personal

19. Of all the customers who stop doing business with organizations, approximately _____ do so because of indifferent treatment by employees.
    A. 20%   B. 45%   C. 70%   D. 95%

20. If a customer service representative is aware that the organization is not capable of meeting a customer's expectations, the representative's FIRST responsibility would be to
    A. tell the customer of the organization's inability to comply
    B. shape the customer's expectations to match what the organization can do as he/she asks
    C. encourage the customer to believe that the organization can do as he/she asks
    D. make the sale on the organization's product

21. The following is an example of a *bonus benefit* associated with a product or service:
    A customer
    A. buys a sporty sedan and finds that its tight turning ratio makes it easy to park
    B. buys bread specifically because he wants to receive a coupon for his next purchase
    C. purchases a car and discovers a strange smell in the upholstery
    D. buys a music audiotape and discovers that there are advertisements at the beginning and end of the tape

22. Approximately _____ of customers who voice complaints with an organization will continue to do business with the organization if the complaint is resolved promptly.
    A. 25   B. 40   C. 75   D. 95

23. Though necessary, a positive, proactive customer satisfaction policy will USUALLY be restricted by costs and
    A. volume of service problems
    B. limitations of management personnel authority
    C. unreasonable customer demands
    D. limitations of service policy

24. According to MOST customers, _____ prevents good listening on the part of a service representative when a customer is speaking.
    A. technological apparatus (e.g., voicemail)
    B. frequent interruptions by other staff or customers
    C. asking unnecessary questions
    D. background noise

25. The ability to provide the promised service or product dependably and accurately maybe defined as
    A. assurance
    B. responsiveness
    C. courtesy
    D. reliability

25.____

KEY (CORRECT ANSWERS)

1.	C		11.	A
2.	B		12.	D
3.	C		13.	D
4.	D		14.	C
5.	B		15.	A
6.	C		16.	B
7.	B		17.	D
8.	C		18.	B
9.	A		19.	C
10.	D		20.	B

21. A
22. D
23. D
24. B
25. D

EXAMINATION SECTION
TEST 1

DIRECTIONS: Each question or incomplete statement is followed by several suggested answers or completions. Select the one that BEST answers the question or completes the statement. *PRINT THE LETTER OF THE CORRECT ANSWER IN THE SPACE AT THE RIGHT.*

1. When conducting a needs assessment for the purpose of education planning, an agency's FIRST step is to identify or provide
    A. a profile of population characteristics
    B. barriers to participation
    C. existing resources
    D. profiles of competing resources

    1.____

2. Research has demonstrated that of the following, the MOST effective medium for communicating with external publics is(are)
    A. video news releases
    B. television
    C. radio
    D. newspapers

    2.____

3. Basic ideas behind the effort to influence the attitudes and behaviors of a constituency include each of the following EXCEPT the idea that
    A. words, rather than actions or events, are most likely to motivate
    B. demands for action are a usual response
    C. self-interest usually figures heavily into public involvement
    D. the reliability of change programs is difficult to assess

    3.____

4. An agency representative is trying to craft a pithy message to constituents in order to encourage the use of agency program resources.
Choosing an audience for such messages is easiest when the message
    A. is project- or behavior-based
    B. is combined with other messages
    C. is abstract
    D. has a broad appeal

    4.____

5. Of the following factors, the MOST important to the success of an agency's external education or communication programs is the
    A. amount of resources used to implement them
    B. public's prior experiences with the agency
    C. real value of the program to the public
    D. commitment of the internal audience

    5.____

6. A representative for a state agency is being interviewed by a reporter from a local news network. The representative is being asked to defend a program that is extremely unpopular in certain parts of the municipality.
When a constituency is known to be opposed to a position, the MOST useful communication strategy is to present

    6.____

A. only the arguments that are consistent with constituents' views
B. only the agency's side of the issue
C. both sides of the argument as clearly as possible
D. both sides of the argument, omitting key information about the opposing position

7. The MOST significant barriers to effective agency community relations include
   I. widespread distrust of communication strategies
   II. the media's "watchdog" stance
   III. public apathy
   IV. statutory opposition

   The CORRECT answer is:
   A. I only   B. I and II   C. II and III   D. III and IV

8. In conducting an education program, many agencies use workshops and seminars in a classroom setting.
   Advantages of classroom-style teaching over other means of educating the public include each of the following, EXCEPT
   A. enabling an instructor to verify learning through testing and interaction with the target audience
   B. enabling hands-on practice and other participatory learning techniques
   C. ability to reach an unlimited number of participants in a given length of time
   D. ability to convey the latest, most up-to-date information

9. The _____ model of community relations is characterized by an attempt to persuade the public to adopt the agency's point of view.
   A. two-way symmetric   B. two-way asymmetric
   C. public information   D. press agency/publicity

10. Important elements of an internal situation analysis include the
    I. list of agency opponents   II. communication audit
    III. updated organizational almanac IV. stakeholder analysis

    The CORRECT answer is:
    A. I and II   B. I, II, and III   C. II and III   D. I, II, III and IV

11. Government agency information efforts typically involve each of the following objectives, EXCEPT to
    A. implement changes in the policies of government agencies to align with public opinion
    B. communicate the work of agencies
    C. explain agency techniques in a way that invites input from citizens
    D. provide citizen feedback to government administrators

12. Factors that are likely to influence the effectiveness of an educational campaign include the
    I. level of homogeneity among intended participants
    II. number and types of media used
    III. receptivity of the intended participants
    IV. level of specificity in the message or behavior to be taught

    The CORRECT answer is:
    A. I and II   B. I, II, and III   C. II and III   D. I, II, III, and IV

13. An agency representative is writing instructional objectives that will later help to measure the effectiveness of an educational program.
    Which of the following verbs, included in an objective, would be MOST helpful for the purpose of measuring effectiveness?
    A. Know   B. Identify   C. Learn   D. Comprehend

14. A state education agency wants to encourage participation in a program that has just received a boost through new federal legislation. The program is intended to include participants from a wide variety of socioeconomic and other demographic characteristics. The agency wants to launch a broad-based program that will inform virtually every interested party in the state about the program's new circumstances.
    In attempting to deliver this message to such a wide-ranging constituency, the agency's BEST practice would be to
    A. broadcast the same message through as many different media channels as possible
    B. focus on one discrete segment of the public at a time
    C. craft a message whose appeal is as broad as the public itself
    D. let the program's achievements speak for themselves and rely on word-of-mouth

15. Advantages associated with using the World Wide Web as an educational tool include
    I. an appeal to younger generations of the public
    II. visually-oriented, interactive learning
    III. learning that is not confined by space, time, or institutional association
    IV. a variety of methods for verifying use and learning

    The CORRECT answer is:
    A. I only   B. I and II   C. I, II, and III   D. I, II, II, and IV

16. In agencies involved in health care, community relations is a critical function because it
    A. serves as an intermediary between the agency and consumers
    B. generates a clear mission statement for agency goals and priorities
    C. ensures patient privacy while satisfying the media's right to information
    D. helps marketing professionals determine the wants and needs of agency constituents

17. After an extensive campaign to promote its newest program to constituents, an agency learns that most of the audience did not understand the intended message.
MOST likely, the agency has
   A. chosen words that were intended to inform, rather than persuade
   B. not accurately interpreted what the audience really needed to know
   C. overestimated the ability of the audience to receive and process the message
   D. compensated for noise that may have interrupted the message

18. The necessary elements that lead to conviction and motivation in the minds of participants in an educational or information program include each of the following, EXCEPT the _____ of the message.
   A. acceptability
   B. intensity
   C. single-channel appeal
   D. pervasiveness

19. Printed materials are often at the core of educational programs provided by public agencies.
The PRIMARY disadvantage associated with print is that it
   A. does not enable comprehensive treatment of a topic
   B. is generally unreliable in term of assessing results
   C. is often the most expensive medium available
   D. is constrained by time

20. Traditional thinking on public opinion holds that there is about _____ percent of the public who are pivotal to shifting the balance and momentum of opinion—they are concerned about an issue, but not fanatical, and interested enough to pay attention to a reasoned discussion.
   A. 2
   B. 10
   C. 33
   D. 51

21. One of the most useful guidelines for influencing attitude change among people is to
   A. invite the target audience to come to you, rather than approaching them
   B. use moral appeals as the primary approach
   C. use concrete images to enable people to see the results of behaviors or indifference
   D. offer tangible rewards to people for changes in behavior

22. An agency is attempting to evaluate the effectiveness of its educational program. For this purpose, it wants to observe several focus groups discussing the same program.
Which of the following would NOT be a guideline for the use of focus groups?
   A. Focus groups should only include those who have participated in the program.
   B. Be sure to accurately record the discussion.
   C. The same questions should be asked at each focus group meeting.
   D. It is often helpful to have a neutral, non-agency employee facilitate discussions.

23. Research consistently shows that _____ is the determinant most likely to make a newspaper editor run a news release.
    A. novelty   B. prominence   C. proximity   D. conflict

24. Which of the following is NOT one of the major variables to take into account when considering a population-needs assessment?
    A. State of program development   B. Resources available
    C. Demographics   D. Community attitudes

25. The FIRST step in any communications audit is to
    A. develop a research instrument
    B. determine how the organization currently communicates
    C. hire a contractor
    D. determine which audience to assess

KEY (CORRECT ANSWERS)

1.	A		11.	A
2.	D		12.	D
3.	A		13.	B
4.	A		14.	B
5.	D		15.	C
6.	C		16.	A
7.	D		17.	B
8.	C		18.	C
9.	B		19.	B
10.	C		20.	B

21. C
22. A
23. C
24. C
25. D

TEST 2

DIRECTIONS: Each question or incomplete statement is followed by several suggested answers or completions. Select the one that BEST answers the question or completes the statement. *PRINT THE LETTER OF THE CORRECT ANSWER IN THE SPACE AT THE RIGHT.*

1. A public relations practitioner at an agency has just composed a press release highlighting a program's recent accomplishments and success stories.
   In pitching such releases to print outlets, the practitioner should
   I. e-mail, mail, or send them by messenger
   II. address them to "editor" or "news director"
   III. have an assistant call all media contacts by telephone
   IV. ask reporters or editors how they prefer to receive them

   The CORRECT answer is:
   A. I and II   B. I and IV   C. II, III, and IV   D. III only

   1.____

2. The "output goals" of an educational program are MOST likely to include
   A. specified ratings of services by participants on a standardized scale
   B. observable effects on a given community or clientele
   C. the number of instructional hours provided
   D. the number of participants served

   2.____

3. An agency wants to evaluate satisfaction levels among program participants, and mails out questionnaires to everyone who has been enrolled in the last year.
   The PRIMARY problem associated with this method of evaluative research is that it
   A. poses a significant inconvenience for respondents
   B. is inordinately expensive
   C. does not allow for follow-up or clarification questions
   D. usually involves a low response rate

   3.____

4. A communications audit is an important tool for measuring
   A. the depth of penetration of a particular message or program
   B. the cost of the organization's information campaigns
   C. how key audiences perceive an organization
   D. the commitment of internal stakeholders

   4.____

5. The "ABCs" of written learning objectives include each of the following, EXCEPT
   A. Audience   B. Behavior   C. Conditions   D. Delineation

   5.____

2 (#2)

6. When attempting to change the behaviors of constituents, it is important to keep in mind that
   I. most people are skeptical of communications that try to get them to change their behaviors
   II. in most cases, a person selects the media to which he exposes himself
   III. people tend to react defensively to messages or programs that rely on fear as a motivating factor
   IV. programs should aim for the broadest appeal possible in order to include as many participants as possible

   The CORRECT answer is:
   A. I and II   B. I, II and III   C. II and III   D. I, II, III, and IV

6.____

7. The "laws" of public opinion include the idea that it is
   A. useful for anticipating emergencies
   B. not sensitive to important events
   C. basically determined by self-interest
   D. sustainable through persistent appeals

7.____

8. Which of the following types of evaluations is used to measure public attitudes before and after an information/educational program?
   A. Retrieval study   B. Copy test
   C. Quota sampling   D. Benchmark study

8.____

9. The PRIMARY source for internal communications is(are) usually
   A. flow charts   B. meetings
   C. voice mail   D. printed publications

9.____

10. An agency representative is putting together informational materials—brochures and a newsletter—outlining changes in one of the state's biggest benefits programs.
    In assembling print materials as a medium for delivering information to the public, the representative should keep in mind each of the following trends:
    I. For various reasons, the reading capabilities of the public are in general decline
    II. Without tables and graphs to help illustrate the changes, it is unlikely that the message will be delivered effectively
    III. Professionals and career-oriented people are highly receptive to information written in the form of a journal article or empirical study
    IV. People tend to be put off by print materials that use itemized and bulleted (●) lists

    The CORRECT answer is:
    A. I and II   B. I, II and III   C. II and III   D. I, II, III, and IV

10.____

11. Which of the following steps in a problem-oriented information campaign would typically be implemented FIRST?
    A. Deciding on tactics
    B. Determining a communications strategy
    C. Evaluating the problem's impact
    D. Developing an organizational strategy

11.____

12. A common pitfall in conducting an educational program is to
    A. aim it at the wrong target audience
    B. overfund it
    C. leave it in the hands of people who are in the business of education, rather than those with expertise in the business of the organization
    D. ignore the possibility that some other organization is meeting the same educational need for the target audience

12.____

13. The key factors that affect the credibility of an agency's educational program include
    A. organization   B. scope
    C. sophistication   D. penetration

13.____

14. Research on public opinion consistently demonstrates that it is
    A. easy to move people toward a strong opinion on anything, as long as they are approached directly through their emotions
    B. easier to move people away from an opinion they currently hold than to have them form an opinion about something they have not previously cared about
    C. easy to move people toward a strong opinion on anything, as long as the message appeals to their reason and intellect
    D. difficult to move people toward a strong opinion on anything, no matter what the approach

14.____

15. In conducting an education program, many agencies use meetings and conferences to educate an audience about the organization and its programs. Advantages associated with this approach include
    I. a captive audience that is known to be interested in the topic
    II. ample opportunities for verifying learning
    III. cost-efficient meeting space
    IV. the ability to provide information on a wider variety of subjects

    The CORRECT answer is:
    A. I and II   B. I, III and IV   C. II and III   D. I, II, III and IV

15.____

16. An agency is attempting to evaluate the effectiveness of its educational programs. For this purpose, it wants to observe several focus groups discussing particular programs.
    For this purpose, a focus group should never number more than _____ participants.
    A. 5   B. 10   C. 15   D. 20

16.____

17. A _____ speech is written so that several agency members can deliver it to different audiences with only minor variations.
    A. basic B. printed C. quota D. pattern

18. Which of the following statements about public opinion is generally considered to be FALSE?
    A. Opinion is primarily reactive rather than proactive.
    B. People have more opinions about goals than about the means by which to achieve them.
    C. Facts tend to shift opinion in the accepted direction when opinion is not solidly structured.
    D. Public opinion is based more on information than desire.

19. An agency is trying to promote its educational program.
    As a general rule, the agency should NOT assume that
    A. people will only participate if they perceive an individual benefit
    B. promotions need to be aimed at small, discrete groups
    C. if the program is good, the audience will find out about it
    D. a variety of methods, including advertising, special events, and direct mail, should be considered

20. In planning a successful educational program, probably the first and most important question for an agency to ask is:
    A. What will be the content of the program?
    B. Who will be served by the program?
    C. When is the best time to schedule the program?
    D. Why is the program necessary?

21. Media kits are LEAST likely to contain
    A. fact sheets   B. memoranda
    C. photographs with captions D. news releases

22. The use of pamphlets and booklets as media for communication with the public often involves the disadvantage that
    A. the messages contained within them are frequently nonspecific
    B. it is difficult to measure their effectiveness in delivering the message
    C. there are few opportunities for people to refer to them
    D. color reproduction is poor

23. The MOST important prerequisite of a good educational program is an
    A. abundance of resources to implement it
    B. individual staff unit formed for the purpose of program delivery
    C. accurate needs assessment
    D. uneducated constituency

24. After an education program has been delivered, an agency conducts a program evaluation to determine whether its objectives have been met.
General rules about how to conduct such an education program valuation include each of the following, EXCEPT that it
    A. must be done immediately after the program has been implemented
    B. should be simple and easy to use
    C. should be designed so that tabulation of responses can take place quickly and inexpensively
    D. should solicit mostly subjective, open-ended responses if the audience was large

25. Using electronic media such as television as means of educating the public is typically recommended ONLY for agencies that
    I. have a fairly simple message to begin with
    II. want to reach the masses, rather than a targeted audience
    III. have substantial financial resources
    IV. accept that they will not be able to measure the results of the campaign with much precision

    The CORRECT answer is:
    A. I and II   B. I, II and III   C. II and IV   D. I, II, III and IV

KEY (CORRECT ANSWERS)

1.	B		11.	C
2.	C		12.	D
3.	D		13.	A
4.	C		14.	D
5.	D		15.	B
6.	B		16.	B
7.	C		17.	D
8.	D		18.	D
9.	D		19.	C
10.	A		20.	D

21.	B
22.	B
23.	C
24.	D
25.	D

READING COMPREHENSION
UNDERSTANDING AND INTERPRETING WRITTEN MATERIAL

EXAMINATION SECTION

TEST 1

DIRECTIONS: Each question or incomplete statement is followed by several suggested answers or completions. Select the one that BEST answers the question or completes the statement. *PRINT THE LETTER OF THE CORRECT ANSWER IN THE SPACE AT THE RIGHT.*

Questions 1-3.

DIRECTIONS: Questions 1 through 3 are to be answered SOLELY on the basis of the following passage.

Every organization needs a systematic method of checking its operations as a means to increase efficiency and promote economy. Many successful private firms have instituted a system of audit or internal inspections to accomplish these ends. Law enforcement organizations, which have an extremely important service to *sell*, should be no less zealous in developing efficiency and economy in their operations. Periodic, organized, and systematic inspections are one means of promoting the achievement of these objectives. The necessity of an organized inspection system is perhaps greatest in those law enforcement groups which have grown to such a size that the principal officer can no longer personally supervise or be cognizant of every action taken. Smooth and effective operation demands that the head of the organization have at hand some tool with which he can study and enforce general policies and procedure and also direct compliance with day-to-day orders, most of which are put into execution outside his sight and hearing. A good inspection system can serve as that tool.

1. The central thought of the above passage is that a system of inspections within a police department
   A. is unnecessary for a department in which the principal officer can personally supervise all official actions taken
   B. should be instituted at the first indication that there is any deterioration in job performance by the force
   C. should be decentralized and administered by first-line supervisory officers
   D. is an important aid to the police administrator in the accomplishment of law enforcement objectives

1.____

2. The MOST accurate of the following statements concerning the need for an organized inspection system in a law enforcement organization is: It is
   A. never needed in an organization of small size where the principal officer can give personal supervision
   B. most needed where the size of the organization prevents direct supervision by the principal officer
   C. more needed in law enforcement organizations than in private firms
   D. especially needed in an organization about to embark upon a needed expansion of services

2.____

3. According to the above passage, the head of the police organization utilizes the internal inspection system
   A. as a tool which must be constantly re-examined in the light of changing demands for police service
   B. as an administrative technique to increase efficiency and promote economy
   C. by personally visiting those areas of police operation which are outside his sight and hearing
   D. to augment the control of local commanders over detailed field operations

3._____

Questions 4-10.

DIRECTIONS: Questions 4 through 10 are to be answered SOLELY on the basis of the following passage.

Job evaluation and job rating systems are intended to introduce scientific procedures. Any type of approach, when properly used, will give satisfactory results. The Point System, when properly validated by actual use, is more likely to be suitable for general use than the ranking system. In many aspects, the Factor Comparison Plan is a point system tied to money values. Of course, there may be another system that combines the ranking system with the point system, especially during the initial stages of the development of the program. After the program has been in use for some time, the tendency is to drop off the ranking phase and continue the use of the point system.

In the ranking system of rating of jobs, every job within the plant is arranged in some order, either from the one with the simplest qualifications to the one with maximum requirements, or in the reverse order. This system should be preceded by careful job analysis and the writing of accurate job descriptions before the rating process is undertaken. It is possible, of course, to take the jobs as they are found in the business enterprise and use the names as they are without any attempt at standardization, and merely rank them according to the general overall impression of the raters. Such a procedure is certain to fall short of what may reasonably be expected of job rating. Another procedure that is in reality merely a modification of the simple rating described above is to establish a series of grades or zones and arrange all he jobs in the plant into groups within these grades and zones. The practice in most common use is to arrange all the jobs in the plant according to their requirements by rating them and then to establish the classification or groups.

The actual ranking of jobs may be done by one individual, several individuals, or a committee. If several individuals are working independently on the task, it will usually be found that, in general, they agree but that their rankings vary in certain details. A conference between the individuals, with each person giving his reasons why he rated one way or another, usually produces agreement. The detailed job descriptions are particularly helpful when there is disagreement among raters as to the rating of certain jobs. It is not only possible but desirable to have workers participate in the construction of the job description and in rating the job.

4. The MAIN theme of this passage is
   A. the elimination of bias in job rating
   B. the rating of jobs by the ranking system
   C. the need or accuracy in allocating points in the point system
   D. pitfalls to avoid in selecting key jobs in the Factor Comparison Plan

4._____

5. The ranking system of rating jobs consists MAINLY of
   A. attaching a point value to each ratable factor of each job prior to establishing an equitable pay scale
   B. arranging every job in the organization in descending order and then following this up with a job analysis of the key jobs
   C. preparing accurate job descriptions after a job analysis and then arranging all jobs either in ascending or descending order based on job requirements
   D. arbitrarily establishing a hierarchy of job classes and grades and then fitting each job into a specific class and grade based on the opinions of unit supervisors

6. The above passage states that the system of classifying jobs MOST used in an organization is to
   A. organize all jobs in the organization in accordance with their requirements and then create categories or clusters of jobs
   B. classify all jobs in the organization according to the titles and rank by which they are currently known in the organization
   C. establish a pre-arranged series of grades or zones and then fit all jobs into one of the grades or zones
   D. determine the salary currently being paid for each job and then rank the jobs in order according to salary

7. According to the above passage, experience has shown that when a group of raters is assigned to the job evaluation task and each individual rates independently of the others, the raters GENERALLY
   A. *agree* with respect to all aspects of their rankings
   B. *disagree* with respect to all or nearly all aspects of the rankings
   C. *disagree* on overall ratings, but agree on specific rating factors
   D. *agree* on overall rankings, but have some variance in some details

8. The above passage states that the use of a detailed job description is of special value when
   A. employees of an organization have participated in the preliminary step involved in actual preparation of the job description
   B. labor representatives are not participating in ranking of the jobs
   C. an individual rater who is unsure of himself is ranking the jobs
   D. a group of raters is having difficulty reaching unanimity with respect to ranking a certain job

9. A comparison of the various rating systems as described in the above passage shows that
   A. the ranking system is not as appropriate for general use as a properly validated point system
   B. the point system is the same as the Factor Comparison Plan except that it places greater emphasis on money

C. no system is capable of combining the point system and the Factor Comparison Plan
D. the point system will be discontinued last when used in combination with the Factor comparison System

10. The above passage implies that the PRINCIPAL reason for creating job evaluation and rating systems was to help
    A. overcome union opposition to existing salary plans
    B. base wage determination on a more objective and orderly foundation
    C. eliminate personal bias on the part of the trained scientific job evaluators
    D. management determine if it was overpricing the various jobs in the organizational hierarchy

10.____

Questions 11-13.

DIRECTIONS: Questions 11 through 13 are to be answered SOLELY on the basis of the following passage.

The common sense character of the merit system seems so natural to most Americans that many people wonder why it should ever have been inoperative. After all, the American economic system, the most phenomenal the world has ever known, is also founded on a rugged selective process which emphasizes the personal qualities of capacity, industriousness, and productivity. The criteria may not have always been appropriate and competition has not always been fair, but competition there was, and the responsibilities and the rewards—with exceptions, of course—have gone to those who could measure up in terms of intelligence, knowledge, or perseverance. This has been true not only in the economic area, in the money-making process, but also in achievement in the professions and other walks of life.

11. According to the above passage, economic rewards in the United State have
    A. always been based on appropriate, fair criteria
    B. only recently been based on a competitive system
    C. not going to people who compete too ruggedly
    D. usually gone to those people with intelligence, knowledge, and perseverance

11.____

12. According to the above passage, a merit system is
    A. an unfair criterion on which to base rewards
    B. unnatural to anyone who is not American
    C. based only on common sense
    D. based on the same principles as the American economic system

12.____

13. According to the above passage, it is MOST accurate to say that
    A. the United States has always had a civil service merit system
    B. civil service employees are very rugged
    C. the American economic system has always been based on a merit objective
    D. competition is unique to the American way of life

13.____

Questions 14-15.

DIRECTIONS: Questions 14 and 15 are to be answered SOLELY on the basis of the following passage.

In-basket tests are often used to assess managerial potential. The exercise consists of a set of papers that would be likely to be found in the in-basket of an administrator or manager at any given time, and requires the individuals participating in the examination to indicate how they would dispose of each item found in the in-basket. In order to handle the in-basket effectively, they must successfully manage their time, refer and assign some work to subordinates, juggle potentially conflicting appointments and meetings, and arrange for follow-up of problems generated by the items in the in-basket. In other words, the in-basket test is attempting to evaluate the participants' abilities to organize their work, set priorities, delegate, control, and make decisions.

14. According to the above passage, to succeed in an in-basket test, an administrator must
    A. be able to read very quickly
    B. have a great deal of technical knowledge
    C. know when to delegate work
    D. arrange a lot of appointments and meetings

14.____

15. According to the above passage, all of the following abilities are indications of managerial potential EXCEPT the ability to
    A. organize and control
    B. manage time
    C. write effective reports
    D. make appropriate decisions

15.____

Questions 16-19.

DIRECTIONS: Questions 16 through 19 are to be answered SOLELY on the basis of the following passage.

A personnel researcher has at his disposal various approaches for obtaining information, analyzing it, and arriving at conclusions that have value in predicting and affecting the behavior of people at work. The type of method to be used depends on such factors as the nature of the research problem, the available data, and the attitudes of those people being studied to the various kinds of approaches. While the experimental approach, with its use of control groups, is the most refined type of study, there are others that are often found useful in personnel research. Surveys, in which the researcher obtains facts on a problem from a variety of sources, are employed in research on wages, fringe benefits, and labor relations. Historical studies are used to trace the development of problems in order to understand them better and to isolate possible causative factors. Case studies are generally developed to explore all the details of a particular problem that is representative of other similar problems. A researcher chooses the most appropriate form of study for the problem he is investigating. He should recognize, however, that the experimental method, commonly referred to as the scientific method, if used validly and reliably, gives the most conclusive results.

16. The above passage discusses several approaches used to obtain information on particular problems.
Which of the following may be MOST reasonably concluded from the passage? A(n)
    A. historical study cannot determine causative factors
    B. survey is often used in research on fringe benefits
    C. case study is usually used to explore a problem that is unique and unrelated to other problems
    D. experimental study is used when the scientific approach to a problem fails

17. According to the above passage, all of the following are factors that may determine the type of approach a researcher uses EXCEPT
    A. the attitudes of people toward being used in control groups
    B. the number of available sources
    C. his desire to isolate possible causative factors
    D. the degree of accuracy he requires

18. The words *scientific method*, as used in the last sentence of the above passage, refer to a type of study which, according to the above passage
    A. uses a variety of sources
    B. traces the development of problems
    C. uses control groups
    D. analyzes the details of a representative problem

19. Which of the following can be MOST reasonably concluded from the above passage?
In obtaining and analyzing information on a particular problem, a researcher employs the method which is the
    A. most accurate
    B. most suitable
    C. least expensive
    D. least time-consuming

Questions 20-25.

DIRECTIONS: Questions 20 through 25 are to be answered SOLELY on the basis of the following passage.

The quality of the voice of a worker is an important factor in conveying to clients and co-workers his attitude and, to some degree, his character. The human voice, when not consciously disguised, may reflect a person's mood, temper, and personality. It has been shown in several experiments that certain character traits can be assessed with better than chance accuracy through listening to the voice of an unknown person who cannot be seen.
Since one of the objectives of the worker is to put clients at ease and to present an encouraging and comfortable atmosphere, a harsh, shrill, or loud voice could have a negative effect. A client who displays emotions of anger or resentment would probably be provoked even further by a caustic tone. In a face-to-face situation, an unpleasant voice may be compensated for, to some degree, by a concerned and kind facial expression. However, when one speaks on the telephone, the expression on one's face cannot be seen by the listener. A supervising clerk who wishes to represent himself effectively to clients should try to eliminate as many faults as possible in striving to develop desirable voice qualities.

20. If a worker uses a sarcastic tone while interviewing a resentful client, the client, according to the above passage, would MOST likely
    A. avoid the face-to-face problem
    B. be ashamed of his behavior
    C. become more resentful
    D. be provoked to violence

21. According to the passage, experiments comparing voice and character traits have demonstrated that
    A. prospects for improving an unpleasant voice through training are better than chance
    B. the voice can be altered to project many different psychological characteristics
    C. the quality of the human voice reveals more about the speaker than his words do
    D. the speaker's voice tells the hearer something about the speaker's personality

22. Which of the following, according to the above passage, is a person's voice MOST likely to reveal?
    His
    A. prejudices
    B. intelligence
    C. social awareness
    D. temperament

23. It may be MOST reasonably concluded from the above passage that an interested and sympathetic expression on the face of a worker
    A. may induce a client to feel certain he will receive welfare benefits
    B. will eliminate the need for pleasant vocal qualities in the interviewer
    C. may help to make up for an unpleasant voice in the interviewer
    D. is desirable as the interviewer speaks on the telephone to a client

24. Of the following, the MOST reasonable implication of the above paragraph is that a worker should, when speaking to a client, control and use his voice to
    A. simulate a feeling of interest in the problems of the client
    B. express his emotions directly and adequately
    C. help produce in the client a sense of comfort and security
    D. reflect his own true personality

25. It may be concluded from the above passage that the PARTICULAR reason for a worker to pay special attention to modulating her voice when talking on the phone to a client is that, during a telephone conversation
    A. there is a necessity to compensate for the way in which a telephone distorts the voice
    B. the voice of the worker is a reflection of her mood and character
    C. the client can react only on the basis of the voice and words she hears
    D. the client may have difficulty getting a clear understanding over the telephone

KEY (CORRECT ANSWERS)

1.	D	11.	D
2.	B	12.	D
3.	B	13.	C
4.	B	14.	C
5.	C	15.	C
6.	A	16.	B
7.	D	17.	D
8.	D	18.	C
9.	A	19.	B
10.	B	20.	C

21.	D
22.	D
23.	C
24.	C
25.	C

TEST 2

DIRECTIONS: Each question or incomplete statement is followed by several suggested answers or completions. Select the one that BEST answers the question or completes the statement. *PRINT THE LETTER OF THE CORRECT ANSWER IN THE SPACE AT THE RIGHT.*

Questions 1-3.

DIRECTIONS: Questions 1 through 3 are to be answered SOLELY on the basis of the following paragraph.

Suppose you are given the job of printing, collating, and stapling 8,000 copies of a ten-page booklet as soon as possible. You have available one photo-offset machine, a collator with an automatic stapler, and the personnel to operate these machines. All will be available for however long the job takes to complete. The photo-offset machine prints 5,000 impressions an hour, and it takes about 15 minutes to set up a plate. The collator, including time for insertion of pages and stapling, can process about 2,000 booklets an hour. (Answers should be based on the assumption that there are no breakdowns or delays.)

1. Assuming that all the printing is finished before the collating is started, if the job is given to you late Monday and your section can begin work the next day and is able to devote seven hours a day, Monday through Friday, to the job until it is finished, what is the BEST estimate of when the job will be finished?
    A. Wednesday afternoon of the same week
    B. Thursday morning of the same week
    C. Friday morning of the same week
    D. Monday morning of the next week

1.____

2. An operator suggests to you that instead of completing all the printing and then beginning collating and stapling, you first print all the pages for 4,000 booklets, so that they can be collated and stapled while the last 4,000 pages are being printed.
If you accepted this suggestion, the job would be completed
    A. sooner but would require more man-hours
    B at the same time using either method
    C. later and would require more man-hours
    D. sooner but there would be more wear and tear on the plates

2.____

3. Assume that you have the same assignment and equipment as described above, but 16,000 copies of the booklet are needed instead of 8,000.
If you decided to print 8,000 complete booklets, then collate and staple them while you started printing the next 8,000 booklets, which of the following statements would MOST accurately describe the relationship between this new method and your original method of printing all the booklets at one time, and then collating and stapling them? The
    A. job would be completed at the same time regardless of the method used
    B. new method would result in the job's being completed 3½ hours earlier
    C. original method would result in the job's being completed an hour later
    D. new method would result in the job's being completed 1½ hours earlier

3.____

Questions 4-6.

DIRECTIONS: Questions 4 through 6 are to be answered SOLELY on the basis of the following passage.

When using words like company, association, council, committee, and board in place of the full official name, the writer should not capitalize these short forms unless he intends them to invoke the full force of the institution's authority. In legal contracts, in minutes, or in formal correspondence where one is speaking formally and officially on behalf of the company, the term Company is usually capitalized, but in ordinary usage, where it is not essential to load the short form with this significance, capitalization would be excessive. (Example: The company will have many good openings for graduates this June.)

The treatment recommended for short forms of place names is essentially the same as that recommended for short forms of organizational names. In general, we capitalize the full form but not the short form. If Park Avenue is referred to in one sentence, then the *avenue* is sufficient in subsequent references. The same is true with words like building, hotel, station, and airport, which are capitalized when part of a proper name changed (Pan Am Building, Hotel Plaza, Union Station, O'Hare Airport), but are simply lower-cased when replacing these specific names.

4. The above passage states that USUALLY the short forms of names of organizations
   A. and places should not be capitalized
   B. and places should be capitalized
   C. should not be capitalized, but the short forms of names of places should be capitalized
   D. should be capitalized, but the short forms of names of places should not be capitalized

5. The above passage states that in legal contracts, in minutes, and in formal correspondence, the short forms of names of organizations should
   A. usually not be capitalized
   B. usually be capitalized
   C. usually not be used
   D. never be used

6. It can be inferred from the above passage that decisions regarding when to capitalize certain words
   A. should be left to the discretion of the writer
   B. should be based on generally accepted rules
   C. depend on the total number of words capitalized
   D. are of minor importance

Questions 7-10.

DIRECTIONS: Questions 7 through 10 are to be answered SOLELY on the basis of the following passage.

Use of the systems and procedures approach to office management is revolutionizing the supervision of office work. This approach views an enterprise as an entity which seeks to fulfill definite objectives. Systems and procedures help to organize repetitive work into a routine, thus reducing the amount of decision making required for its accomplishment. As a result, employees are guided in their efforts and perform only necessary work. Supervisors are relieved of any details of execution and are free to attend to more important work. Establishing work guides which require that identical tasks be performed the same way each time permits standardization of forms, machine operations, work methods, and controls. This approach also reduces the probability of errors. Any error committed is usually discovered quickly because the incorrect work does not meet the requirement of the work guides. Errors are also reduced through work specialization, which allows each employee to become thoroughly proficient in a particular type of work. Such proficiency also tends to improve the morale of the employees.

7. The above passage states that the accuracy of an employee's work is INCREASED by
    A. using the work specialization approach
    B. employing a probability sample
    C. requiring him to shift at one time into different types of tasks
    D. having his supervisor check each detail of work execution

8. Of the following, which one BEST expresses the main theme of the above passage? The
    A. advantages and disadvantages of the systems and procedures approach to office management
    B. effectiveness of the systems and procedures approach to office management in developing skills
    C. systems and procedures approach to office management as it relates to office costs
    D. advantages of the systems and procedures approach to office management for supervisors and office workers

9. Work guides are LEAST likely to be used when
    A. standardized forms are used
    B. a particular office task is distinct and different from all others
    C. identical tasks are to be performed in identical ways
    D. similar work methods are expected from each employee

10. According to the above passage, when an employee makes a work error, it USUALLY
    A. is quickly corrected by the supervisor
    B. necessitates a change in the work guides
    C. can be detected quickly if work guides are in use
    D. increases the probability of further errors by that employee

Questions 11-12.

DIRECTIONS: Questions 11 and 12 are to be answered SOLELY on the basis of the following passage.

The coordination of the many activities of a large public agency is absolutely essential. Coordination, as an administrative principle, must be distinguished from and is independent of cooperation. Coordination can be of either the horizontal or the vertical type. In large organizations, the objectives of vertical coordination are achieved by the transmission of orders and statements of policy down through the various levels of authority. It is an accepted generalization that the more authoritarian the organization, the more easily may vertical coordination be accomplished. Horizontal coordination is arrived through staff work, administrative management, and conferences of administrators of equal rank. It is obvious that of the two types of coordination, the vertical kind is more important, for at best horizontal coordination only supplements the coordination effected up and down the line,

11. According to the above passage, the ease with which vertical coordination is achieved in a large agency depends upon
    A. the extent to which control is firmly exercised from above
    B. the objectives that have been established for the agency
    C. the importance attached by employees to the orders and statements of policy transmitted through the agency
    D. the cooperation obtained at the various levels of authority

12. According to the above passage,
    A. vertical coordination is dependent for its success upon horizontal coordination
    B. one type of coordination may work in opposition to the other
    C. similar methods may be used to achieve both types of coordination
    D. horizontal coordination is at most an addition to vertical coordination

Questions 13-17.

DIRECTIONS: Questions 13 through 17 are to be answered SOLELY on the basis of the following situation.

Assume that you are a newly appointed supervisor in the same unit in which you have been acting as a provisional for some time. You have in your unit the following workers:

WORKER I: He has always been an efficient worker. In a number of his cases, the clients have recently begun to complain that they cannot manage on the departmental budget.

WORKER II: He has been under selective supervision for some time as an experienced, competent worker. He now begins to be late for his supervisory conferences and to stress how much work he has to do.

WORKER III: He has been making considerable improvement in his ability to handle the details of his job. He now tells you, during an individual conference, that he does not need such close supervision and that he wants to operate more independently. He says that Worker II is always available when he needs a little information or help but, in general, he can manage very well by himself.

5 (#2)

WORKER IV: He brings you a complex case for decision as to eligibility. Discussion of the case brings out the fact that he has failed to consider all the available resources adequately but has stressed the family's needs to include every extra item in the budget. This is the third case of a similar nature that his worker has brought to you recently. This worker and Worker I work in adjacent territory and are rather friendly.

In the following questions, select the option that describes the method of dealing with these workers that illustrate BEST supervisory practice.

13. With respect to supervision of Worker I, the assistant supervisor should 13.____
    A. discuss with the worker, in an individual conference, any problems that he may be having due to the increase in the cost of living
    B. plan a group conference for the unit around budgeting, as both Workers I and IV seem to be having budgetary difficulties
    C. discuss with Workers I and IV together the meaning of money as acceptance or rejection to the clients
    D. discuss with Worker I the budgetary data in each case in relation to each client's situation

14. With respect to supervision of Worker II, the supervisory should 14.____
    A. move slowly with this worker and give him time to learn that the supervisor's official appointment has not changed his attitudes or methods of supervision
    B. discuss the worker's change of attitude and asks him to analyze the reasons for his change in behavior
    C. take time to show the worker how he is avoiding his responsibility in the supervisor-worker relationship and that he is resisting supervision
    D. hold an evaluatory conference with the worker and show him how he is taking over responsibilities that are not his by providing supervision for Worker III

15. With respect to supervision of Worker III, the supervisor should discuss with this worker 15.____
    A. why he would rather have supervision from Worker II than from the supervisor
    B. the necessity for further improvement before he can go on selective supervision
    C. an analysis of the improvement that has been made and the extent to which the worker is able to handle the total job for which he is responsible
    D. the responsibility of the supervisor to see that clients receive adequate service

16. With respect to supervision of Worker IV, the supervisor should 16.____
    A. show the worker that resources figures are incomplete but that even if they were complete, the family would probably be eligible for assistance
    B. ask the worker why he is so protective of these families since there are three cases so similar

C. discuss with the worker all three cases at the same time so that the worker may see his own role in the three situations
D. discuss with the worker the reasons for departmental policies and procedures around budgeting

17. With respect to supervision of Workers I and IV, since these two workers are friends and would seem to be influencing each other, the supervisor should
    A. hold a joint conference with them both, pointing out how they should clear with the supervisor and not make their own rules together
    B. handle the problems of each separately in individual conferences
    C. separate them by transferring one to another territory or another unit
    D. take up the problem of workers asking help of each other rather than from the supervisor in a group meeting

17.____

Questions 18-20.

DIRECTIONS: Questions 18 through 20 are to be answered SOLELY on the basis of the following passage.

One of the key supervisory problems in a large municipal recreation department is that many leaders are assigned to isolated playgrounds or small centers, where it is difficult to observe their work regularly. Often their facilities are extremely limited. In such settings, as well as in larger recreation centers, where many recreation leaders tend to have other jobs as well, there tends to be a low level of morale and incentive. Still, it is the supervisor's task to help recreation personnel to develop pride in their work and to maintain a high level of performance. With isolated leaders, the supervisor may give advice or assistance. Leaders may be assigned to different tasks or settings during the year to maximize their productivity and provide new challenges. When it is clear that leaders are no willing to make a real effort to contribute to the department, the possibility of penalties must be considered, within the scope of departmental policy and the union contract. However, the supervisor should be constructive, encourage and assist workers to take a greater interest in their work, be innovative, and try to raise morale and to improve performance in positive ways.

18. The one of the following that would the MOST appropriate title for the above passage is
    A. Small Community Centers – Pro and Con
    B. Planning Better Recreation Programs
    C. The Supervisor's Task in Upgrading Personnel Performance
    D. The Supervisor and the Municipal Union – Rights and Obligations

18.____

19. The above passage makes clear that recreation leadership performance in all recreation playgrounds and centers throughout a large city is
    A. generally above average, with good morale on the part of most recreation leaders
    B. beyond description since no one has ever observed or evaluated recreation leaders

19.____

C. a key test of the personnel department's effort to develop more effective hiring standards
D. of mixed quality, with many recreation leaders having poor morale and a low level of achievement

20. According to the above passage, the supervisor's role is to
    A. use disciplinary action as his major tool in upgrading performance
    B. tolerate the lack of effort of individual employees since they are assigned to isolated playgrounds or small centers
    C. employ encouragement, advice, and, when appropriate, disciplinary action to improve performance
    D. inform the county supervisor whenever malfeasance or idleness is detected

Questions 21-25.

DIRECTIONS: Questions 21 through 25 are to be answered SOLELY on the basis of the following passage.

EMPLOYEE LEAVE REGULATIONS

Peter Smith, as a full-time permanent city employee under the Career and Salary Plan, earns an *annual leave allowance*. This consists of a certain number of days off a year with pay and may be used for vacation, personal business, and for observing religious holidays. As a newly appointed employee, during his first 8 years of city service, he will earn an annual leave allowance of 20 days off a year (an average of $1^2/_3$ days off a month). After he has finished 8 full years of working for the city, he will begin earning an additional 5 days off a year. His annual leave allowance, therefore, will then be 25 days a year and will remain at this amount for seven full years. He will begin earning an additional two days off a year at this amount for seven full years. He will begin earning an additional two days off a year after he has completed a total of 15 years of city employment. Therefore, in his sixteenth year of working for the city, Mr. Smith will be earning 27 days off a year as his annual leave allowance (an average of 2¼ days off a month).

A *sick leave allowance* of one day a month is also given to Mr. Smith, but it can be used only in cases of actual illness. When Mr. Smith returns to work after using sick leave allowance, he must have a doctor's note if the absence is for a total of more than 3 days, but he may also be required to show a doctor's note for absences of 1, 2, or 3 days.

21. According to the above passage, Mr. Smith's annual leave allowance consists of a certain number of days off a year which he
    A. does not get paid for
    B. gets paid for at time and a half
    C. may use for personal business
    D. may not use for observing religious holidays

22. According to the above passage, after Mr. Smith has been working for the city for 9 years, his annual leave allowance will be _____ days a year.
    A. 20   B. 25   C. 27   D. 37

8 (#2)

23. According to the above passage, Mr. Smith will begin earning an average of 2 days off a month as his annual leave allowance after he has worked for the city for _____ full years.   23.____
    A. 7   B. 8   C. 15   D. 17

24. According to the above passage, Mr. Smith is given a sick leave allowance of   24.____
    A. 1 day every 2 months   B. 1 day per month
    C. $1\frac{2}{3}$ days per month   D. 2¼ days a month

25. According to the above passage, when he uses sick leave allowance, Mr. Smith may be required to show a doctor's note   25.____
    A. even if his absence is for only 1 day
    B. only if his absence is for more than 2 days
    C. only if his absence is for more than 3 days
    D. only if his absence is for 3 days or more

KEY (CORRECT ANSWERS)

1.	C		11.	A
2.	C		12.	D
3.	D		13.	D
4.	A		14.	A
5.	B		15.	C
6.	B		16.	C
7.	A		17.	B
8.	D		18.	C
9.	B		19.	D
10.	C		20.	C

21.	C
22.	B
23.	C
24.	B
25.	A

TEST 3

DIRECTIONS: Each question or incomplete statement is followed by several suggested answers or completions. Select the one that BEST answers the question or completes the statement. *PRINT THE LETTER OF THE CORRECT ANSWER IN THE SPACE AT THE RIGHT.*

Questions 1-6.

DIRECTIONS: Questions 1 through 6 are to be answered SOLELY on the basis of the following passage.

    A folder is made of a sheet of heavy paper (manila, kraft, pressboard, or red rope stock) that has been folded once so that the back is about one-half inch higher than the front. Folders are larger than the papers they contain in order to protect them. Two standard folder sizes are *letter size* for papers that are 8½" x 11" and *legal cap* for papers that are 8½" x 13".
    Folders are cut across the top in two ways: so that the back is straight (straight-cut) or so that the back has a tab that projects above the top of the folder. Such tabs bear captions that identify the contents of each folder. Tabs vary in width and position. The tabs of a set of folders that are *one-half cut* are half the width of the folder and have only two positions.
    One-third cut folders have three positions, each tab occupying a third of the width of the folder. Another standard tabbing is *one-fifth cut*, which has five positions. There are also folders with *two-fifths cut*, with the tabs in the third and fourth or fourth and fifth positions.

1. Of the following, the BEST title for the above passage is
    A. Filing Folders
    B. Standard Folder Sizes
    C. The Uses of the Folder
    D. The Use of Tabs

2. According to the above passage, one of the standard folder sizes is called
    A. Kraft cut
    B. legal cap
    C. one-half cut
    D. straight-cut

3. According to the above passage, tabs are GENERALLY placed along the _____ of the folder.
    A. back   B. front   C. left side   D. right side

4. According to the above passage, a tab is GENERALLY used to
    A. distinguish between standard folder sizes
    B. identify the contents of a folder
    C. increase the size of the folder
    D. protect the papers within the folder

5. According to the above passage, a folder that is two-fifths cut has _____ tabs.
    A. no   B. two   C. three   D. five

6. According to the above passage, one reason for making folders larger than the papers they contain is that
   A. only a certain size folder can be made from heavy paper
   B. they will protect the papers
   C. they will aid in setting up a tab system
   D. the back of the folder must be higher than the front

Questions 7-15.

DIRECTIONS: Questions 7 through 15 are to be answered SOLELY on the basis of the following passage.

The City University of New York traces its origins to 1847, when the Free Academy, which later became City College, was founded as the first tuition-free municipal college. City and Hunter Colleges were placed under the direction of the Board of Higher Education in 1926, and Brooklyn and Queens Colleges were subsequently added to the system of municipal colleges. In 1955, Staten Island Community College, the first of the two-year colleges sponsored by the Board of Higher Education under the program of the State University of New York, joined the system.

In 1961, the four senior colleges and three community colleges then under the jurisdiction of the Board of Higher Education became the City University of New York, and a University Graduate Division was organized to offer programs leading to the Ph.D. Since then, the university has undergone even more rapid growth. Today, it consists of nine senior colleges, an upper division college which admits students at the junior level, eight community colleges, a graduate division, and an affiliated medical center.

In the summer of 1969, the Board of Higher Education resolved that the time had come to commit the resources of the university to meeting an urgent social need—unrestricted access to higher education for all youths of the City. Determined to prevent the waste of human potential represented by the thousands of high school graduates whose limited educational opportunities left them unable to meet existing admission standards, the Board moved to adopt a policy of Open Admissions. It was their judgment that the best way of determining whether a potential student can benefit from college work is to admit him to college, provide him with the learning assistance he needs, and then evaluate his performance.

Beginning with the class of June 1970, every New York City resident who received a high school diploma from a public or private high school was guaranteed a place in one of the colleges of City University.

7. Of the following, the BEST title for the above passage is
   A. A Brief History of the City University
   B. High Schools and the City University
   C. The Components of the University
   D. Tuition-free Colleges

8. According to the above passage, which one of the following colleges of the City University was ORIGINALLY called the Free Academy?
   A. Brooklyn College   B. City College
   C. Hunter College   D. Queens College

9. According to the above passage, the system of municipal colleges became the 9.____
City University of New York in
   A. 1926   B. 1955   C. 1961   D. 1969

10. According to the above passage, Staten Island Community College came 10.____
under the jurisdiction of the Board of Higher Education
   A. 6 years after a Graduate Division was organized
   B. 8 years before the adoption of the Open Admissions Policy
   C. 29 years after Brooklyn and Queens Colleges
   D. 29 years after City and Hunter Colleges

11. According to the above passage, the Staten Island Community College is 11.____
   A. a graduate division center   B. a senior college
   C. a two-year college   D. an upper division college

12. According to the above passage, the TOTAL number of colleges, divisions, 12.____
and affiliated branches of the City University is
   A. 18   B. 19   C. 20   D. 21

13. According to the above passage, the Open Admissions Policy is designed 13.____
to determine whether a potential student will benefit from college by
PRIMARILY
   A. discouraging competition for placement in the City University among high
      school students
   B. evaluating his performance after entry into college
   C. lowering admission standards
   D. providing learning assistance before entry into college

14. According to the above passage, the FIRST class to be affected by the Open 14.____
Admissions Policy was the
   A. high school class which graduated in January 1970
   B. City University class which graduated in June 1970
   C. high school class when graduated in June 1970
   D. City University class when graduated in June 1970

15. According to the above passage, one of the reasons that the Board of Higher 15.____
Education initiated the policy of Open Admission was to
   A. enable high school graduates with a background of limited educational
      opportunities to enter college
   B. expand the growth of the City University so as to increase the number
      and variety of degrees offered
   C. provide a social resource to the qualified youth of the City
   D. revise admission standards to meet the needs of the City

Questions 16-18.

DIRECTIONS: Questions 16 through 18 are to be answered SOLELY on the basis of the following passage.

Hereafter, all probationary students interested in transferring to community college career programs (associate degrees) from liberal arts programs in senior colleges (bachelor degrees) will be eligible for such transfers if they have completed no more than three semesters.

For students with averages 1.5 or above, transfer will be automatic. Those with 1.0 to 1.5 averages can transfer provisionally and will be required to make substantial progress during the first semester in the career program. Once transfer has taken place, only those courses in which passing grades were received will be computed in the community college grade-point average.

No request for transfer will be accepted from probationary students wishing to enter the liberal arts programs at the community college.

16. According to the above passage, the one of the following which is the BEST statement concerning the transfer of probationary students is that a probationary student
    A. may transfer to a career program at the end of one semester
    B. must complete three semester hours before he is eligible for transfer
    C. is not eligible to transfer to a career program
    D. is eligible to transfer to a liberal arts program

16.____

17. Which of the following is the BEST statement of academic evaluation for transfer purposes in the case of probationary students?
    A. No probationary student with an average under 1.5 may transfer.
    B. A probationary student with an average of 1.3 may not transfer.
    C. A probationary student with an average of 1.6 may transfer.
    D. A probationary student with an average of .8 may transfer on a provisional basis.

17.____

18. It is MOST likely that, of the following, the next degree sought by one who already holds the Associate in Science degree would be a(n) _____ degree.
    A. Assistantship in Science   B. Associate in Applied Science
    C. Bachelor of Science   D. Doctor of Philosophy

18.____

Questions 19-20.

DIRECTIONS: Questions 19 and 20 are to be answered SOLELY on the basis of the following passage.

Auto: Auto travel requires prior approval by the President and/or appropriate Dean and must be indicated in the *Request for Travel Authorization* form. Employees authorized to use personal autos on official College business will be reimbursed at the rate of 28¢ per mile for the first 500 miles driven and 18¢ per mile for mileage driven in excess of 500 mile. The Comptroller's Office may limit the amount of reimbursement to the expenditure that would have been made if a less expensive mode of transportation (railroad, airplane, bus, etc.) had been utilized. If this occurs, the traveler will have to pick up the excess expenditure as a personal expense.

Tolls, Parking Fees, and Parking Meter Fees are not reimbursable and many not be claimed.

19. Suppose that Professor T gives the office assistant the following memorandum: Used car for official trip to Albany, New York, and return. Distance from New York to Albany is 148 miles. Tolls were $3.50 each way. Parking garage cost $3.00. When preparing the Travel Expense Voucher for Professor T, the figure which should be claimed for transportation is
    A. $120.88   B. $113.88   C. $82.88   D. $51.44

19._____

20. Suppose that Professor V gives the office assistant the following memorandum: Used car for official trip to Pittsburgh, Pennsylvania, and return. Distance from New York to Pittsburgh is 350 miles. Tolls were $3.30, $11.40 going, and $3.30, $2.00 returning.
    When preparing the Travel Expense Voucher for Professor V, the figure which should be claimed for transportation is
    A. $225.40   B. $176.00   C. $127.40   D. $98.00

20._____

Questions 21-25.

DIRECTIONS: Questions 21 through 25 are to be answered SOLELY on the basis of the following passage.

For a period of nearly fifteen years, beginning in the mid-1950's, higher education sustained a phenomenal rate of growth. The factor principally responsible were continuing improvement in the rate of college entrance by high school graduates, a 50 percent increase in the size of the college-age (eighteen to twenty-one) group and—until about 1967—a rapid expansion of university research activity supported by the Federal government.

Today, as one looks ahead to the year 2010, it is apparent that each of these favorable stimuli will either be abated or turn into a negative factor. The rate of growth of the college-age group has already diminished; and from 2000 to 2005, the size of the college-age group has shrunk annually almost as fast as it grew from 1965 to 1970. From 2005 to 2010, this annual decrease will slow down so that by 2010 the age group will be about the same size as it was in 2009. This substantial net decrease in the size of the college-age group (from 1995 to 2010) will dramatically affect college enrollments since, currently, 83 percent of undergraduates are twenty-one and under, and another 11 percent are twenty-to to twenty-four.

21. Which one of the following factors is NOT mentioned in the above passage as contributing to the high rate of growth of higher education?
    A. A large increase in the size of the eighteen to twenty-one age group
    B. The equalization of educational opportunities among socio-economic groups
    C. The Federal budget impact on research and development spending in the higher education sector
    D. The increasing rate at which high school graduates enter college

21._____

22. Based on the information in the above passage, the size of the college-age group in 2010 will be
    A. larger than it was in 2009   B. larger than it was in 1995
    C. smaller than it was in 2005   D. about the same as it was in 2000

22.____

23. According to the above passage, the tremendous rate of growth of higher education started around
    A. 1950   B. 1955   C. 1960   D. 1965

23.____

24. The percentage of undergraduates who are over age 24 is MOST NEARLY
    A. 6%   B. 8%   C. 11%   D. 17%

24.____

25. Which one of the following conclusions can be substantiated by the information given in the above passage?
    A. The college-age group was about the same size in 2000 as it was in 1965.
    B. The annual decrease in the size of the college-age group from 2000 to 2005 is about the same as the annual increase from 1965 to 1970.
    C. The overall decrease in the size of the college-age group from 2000 to 2005 will be followed by an overall increase in its size from 2005 to 2010.
    D. The size of the college-age group is decreasing at a fairly constant rate from 1995 to 2010.

25.____

KEY (CORRECT ANSWERS)

1.	A		11.	C
2.	B		12.	C
3.	A		13.	B
4.	B		14.	C
5.	B		15.	A
6.	B		16.	A
7.	A		17.	C
8.	B		18.	C
9.	C		19.	C
10.	D		20.	B

21. B
22. C
23. B
24. A
25. B

ARITHMETICAL REASONING

EXAMINATION SECTION

TEST 1

DIRECTIONS: Each question or incomplete statement is followed by several suggested answers or completions. Select the one that BEST answers the question or completes the statement. *PRINT THE LETTER OF THE CORRECT ANSWER IN THE SPACE AT THE RIGHT.*

1. The ABC Corporation had a gross income of $125,500.00 in 2019. Of this, it paid 60% for overhead.
   If the gross income for 2020 increased by $6,500 and the cost of overhead increased to 61% of gross income, how much MORE did it pay for overhead in 2020 than in 2019?
   A. $1,320   B. $5,220   C. $7,530   D. $8,052   1.____

2. After one year, Mr. Richards paid back a total of $16,950 as payment for a $15,000 loan. All the money paid over $15,000 was simple interest.
   The interest charge was MOST NEARLY
   A. 13%   B. 11%   C. 9%   D. 7%   2.____

3. A checking account has a balance of $253.36.
   If deposits of $36.95, $210.23, and $7.34 and withdrawals of $117.35, $23.37, and $15.98 are made, what is the NEW balance of the account?
   A. $155.54   B. $351.18   C. $364.58   D. $664.58   3.____

4. In 2020, the W Realty Company spent 27% of its income on rent.
   If it earned $97,254 in 2020, the amount it paid for rent was
   A. $26,258.58   B. 26,348.58   C. $27,248.58   D. $27,358.58   4.____

5. Six percent simple annual interest on $2,436.18 is MOST NEARLY
   A. $145.08   B. $145.17   C. $146.08   D. $146.17   5.____

6. H. Partridge receives a weekly gross salary (before deductions) of $397.50. Through weekly payroll deductions of $13.18, he is paying back a loan he took from his pension fund.
   If other fixed weekly deductions amount to $122.76, how much pay would Mr. Partridge take home over a period of 33 weeks?
   A. $7,631.28   B. $8,250.46   C. $8,631.48   D. $13,117.50   6.____

7. Mr. Robertson is a city employee enrolled in a city retirement system. He has taken out a loan from the retirement fund and is paying it back at the rate of $14.90 every two weeks.
   In eighteen weeks, how much money will he have paid back on the loan?
   A. $268.20   B. $152.80   C. $134.10   D. $67.05   7.____

8. In 2019, The Iridor Book Company had the following expenses: rent, $6,500; overhead, $52,585; inventory, $35,700; and miscellaneous, $1,275.
   If all of these expenses went up 18% in 2020, what would they TOTAL in 2020?
   A. $17,290.80   B. $78,769.20   C. $96,060.00   D. $113,350.80

   8.____

9. Ms. Ranier had a gross salary of $710.72 paid once every two weeks.
   If the deductions from each paycheck are $125.44, $50.26, $12.58, and $2.54, how much money would Ms. Ranier take home in eight weeks?
   A. $2,079.60   B. $2,842.88   C. $4,159.20   D. $5,685.76

   9.____

10. Mr. Martin had a net income of $95,500 in 2019.
    If he spent 34% on rent and household expenses, 3% on house furnishings, 25% on clothes, and 36% on food, how much was left for savings and other expenses?
    A. $980   B. $1,910   C. $3,247   D. $9,800

    10.____

11. Mr. Elsberg can pay back a loan of $1,800 from the city employees' retirement system if he pays back $36.69 every two weeks for two full years.
    At the end of the two years, how much more than the original $1,800 he borrowed will Mr. Elsberg have paid back?
    A. $53.94   B. $107.88   C. $190.79   D. $214.76

    11.____

12. Mr. Nusbaum is a city employee receiving a gross salary (salary before deductions) of $20,800. Every two weeks, the following deductions are taken out of his salary: Federal Income Tax, $162.84; FICA, $44.26; State Tax, $29.2; City Tax, $13.94; Health Insurance, $3.14.
    If Mr. Nusbaum's salary and deductions remained the same for a full calendar year, what would his net salary (gross salary less deductions) be in that year?
    A. $6,596.20   B. $14,198.60   C. $18,745.50   D. $20,546.30

    12.____

13. Add: 8936, 7821, 8953, 4297, 9785, 6579.
    A. 45,371   B. 45,381   C. 46,371   D. 46,381

    13.____

14. Multiply: 987
              867
    A. 854,609   B. 854,729   C. 855,709   D. 855,729

    14.____

15. Divide: 59)321439.0
    A. 5438.1   B. 5447.1   C. 5448.1   D. 5457.1

    15.____

16. Divide: .052)721
    A. 12,648.0   B. 12,648.1   C. 12,649.0   D. 12,649.1

    16.____

17. If the total number of employees in one city agency increased from 1,927 to 2,006 during a certain year, the percentage increase in the number of employees for that year is MOST NEARLY
    A. 4%   B. 5%   C. 6%   D. 7%

    17.____

18. During a single fiscal year, which totaled 248 workdays, one account clerk verified 1,488 purchase vouchers.
    Assuming a normal work week of five days, what is the AVERAGE number of vouchers verified by the account clerk in a one-week period during this fiscal year?
    A. 25　　　B. 30　　　C. 35　　　D. 40

19. Multiplying a number by .75 is the same as
    A. multiplying it by $2/3$
    B. dividing it by $2/3$
    C. multiplying it by $3/4$
    D. dividing it by $3/4$

20. In City Agency A, $2/3$ of the employees are enrolled in a retirement system. City Agency B has the same number of employees as Agency A and 60% of these are enrolled in a retirement system.
    If Agency A has a total of 660 employees, how many MORE employees does it have enrolled in a retirement system than does Agency B?
    A. 36　　　B. 44　　　C. 56　　　D. 66

21. Net worth is equal to assets minus liabilities.
    If, at the end of 2019, a textile company had assets of $98,695.83 and liabilities of $59,238.29, what was its net worth?
    A. $38,478.54　　　B. $38,488.64　　　C. $39,457.54　　　D. $48,557.54

22. Mr. Martin's assets consist of the following: Cash on hand, $5,233.74, Automobile, $3,206.09; Furniture, $4,925.00; Government Bonds, $5,500.00; and House, $36,69.85.
    What are his TOTAL assets?
    A. $54,545.68　　　B. $54,455.68　　　C. $55,455.68　　　D. $55,555.68

23. If Mr. Mitchell has $627.04 in his checking account and then writes three checks for $241.75, $13.24, and $102.97, what will be his new balance?
    A. $257.88　　　B. $269.08　　　C. $357.96　　　D. $369.96

24. An employee's net pay is equal to his total earnings less all deductions.
    If an employee's total earnings in a pay period are $497.05, what is his net pay if he has the following deductions: Federal Income Tax, $18.79; City Tax, $7.25; Pension, $1.88?
    A. $351.17　　　B. $351.07　　　C. $350.17　　　D. $350.07

25. A petty cash fund had an opening balance of $85.75 on December 1. Expenditures of $23.00, $15.65, $5.23, $14.75, and $26.38 were made out of this fund during the first 14 days of the month. Then, on December 17, another $38.50 was added to the fund.
    If additional expenditures of $17.18, $3.29, and $11.64 were made during the remainder of the month, what was the FINAL balance of the petty cash fund at the end of December?
    A. $6.93　　　B. $7.13　　　C. $46.51　　　D. $91.40

KEY (CORRECT ANSWERS)

1.	B	11.	B
2.	A	12.	B
3.	B	13.	C
4.	A	14.	D
5.	D	15.	C
6.	C	16.	D
7.	C	17.	A
8.	D	18.	B
9.	A	19.	C
10.	B	20.	B

21.	C
22.	D
23.	B
24.	D
25.	B

5 (#1)

SOLUTIONS TO PROBLEMS

1. ($132,000)(.61) − ($125,500)(.60) = $5,220

2. Interest = $1,950. As a percent, $1950 ÷ 15,000 = 13%

3. New balance = $253.36 + $36.95 + $210.23 + $7.34 - $117.35 - $23.37 - $15.98 = $351.18

4. Rent = ($97,254)(.27) = $26,258.58

5. ($2,436.18)(.06) ≈ $146.17

6. ($397.50 - $13.18 - $122.76) = $8,631.48

7. ($14.90)($\frac{18}{2}$) = $134.10

8. ($6,500 + $52,585 + $35,700 + $1,275)(1.18) = $113,350.80

9. ($710.72 - $125.44 - $50.26 - $12.58 - $2.54)($\frac{8}{2}$) = $2,079.60

10. (1 - .34 - .03 - .25 - .36) - $1,800 = $107.88

11. (36.69)(52) - $1,800 = $107.88

12. $20,800 − (26)($162.84+$44.26+$29.72+$13.94+$3.14) = $14,198.60

13. 8,936 + 7,821 + 8,953 + 4,297 + 9,785 + 6,579 = 46,371

14. (987)(867) − 855,729

15. 321,439 ÷ 59 ≈ 5,448.1

16. 721 ÷ .057 ≈ 12,649.1

17. (2,006-1,927) ÷ 1,927 ≈ 4%

18. Let x = number of vouchers. Then, $\frac{x}{5} = \frac{1488}{248}$. Solving, x = 30

19. Multiplying by .75 is equivalent to multiplying by $\frac{3}{4}$

20. (660)($\frac{2}{3}$) − (660)(.60) = 44

21. Net worth = $98,695.83 - $59,238.29 = $39,457.54

22. Total Assets = $5,233.74 + $3,206.09 + $4,925.00 + $5,500.00) + $36,690.85 = $55,555.68.

23. New balance = $627.04 - $241.75 - $13.24 - $102.97 = $269.08

24. Net pay = $497.05 - $90.32 - $28.74 - $18.79 - $7.25 - $1.88 = $350.07

25. Final balance = $85.75 - $23.00 - $15.65 - $5.23 - $14.75 - $26.38 + $38.50 - $17.18 - $3.29 - $11.64 = $7.13

TEST 2

DIRECTIONS: Each question or incomplete statement is followed by several suggested answers or completions. Select the one that BEST answers the question or completes the statement. *PRINT THE LETTER OF THE CORRECT ANSWER IN THE SPACE AT THE RIGHT.*

1. The formula for computing base salary is: Earnings equals base gross plus additional gross.
   If an employee's earnings during a particular period are in the amounts of $597.45, $535.92, $639.91, and $552.83, and his base gross salary is $525.50 per paycheck, what is the TOTAL of the additional gross earned by the employee during that period?
   A. $224.11   B. $224.21   C. $224.51   D. $244.11

2. If a lump sum death benefit is paid by the retirement system in an amount equal to 3/7 of an employee's last yearly salary of $13,486.50, the amount of the death benefit paid is MOST NEARLY
   A. $5,749.29   B. $5,759.92   C. $5,779.92   D. $5,977.29

3. Suppose that a member has paid 15 installments on a 28-installment loan. The percentage of the number of installments paid to the retirement system is
   A. 53.57%   B. 53.97%   C. 54.57%   D. 55.37%

4. If an employee takes a 1-month vacation during a calendar year, the percentage of the year during which he works is MOST NEARLY
   A. 90.9%   B. 91.3%   C. 91.6%   D. 92.1%

5. Suppose that an employee took a leave of absence totaling 7 months during a calendar year.
   Assuming the employee did not take any vacation time during the remainder of that year, the percentage of the year in which he worked is MOST NEARLY
   A. 41.7%   B. 43.3%   C. 46.5%   D. 47.1%

6. A member has borrowed $4,725 from her funds in the retirement system. If $3,213 has been repaid, the percentage of the loan which is still outstanding is MOST NEARLY
   A. 16%   B. 32%   C. 48%   D. 68%

7. If an employee worked only 24 weeks during the year because of illness, the portion of the year he was out of work was MOST NEARLY
   A. 46%   B. 48%   C. 51%   D. 54%

8. If an employee purchased credit for a 16-week period of service which he had prior to rejoining the retirement system, the percentage of a year he purchased credit for was MOST NEARLY
   A. 27.9%   B. 28.8%   C. 30.7%   D. 33.3%

9. If an employee contributes 2/11 of his yearly salary to his pension fund account, the percentage of his yearly salary which he contributes is MOST NEARLY
   A. 17.9%   B. 18.2%   C. 18.4%   D. 19.0%

10. In 2018, the maximum amount of income from which social security tax could be withheld (base salary) was $70,500. In 2020, the base salary was $82,500. The 2020 base salary represents a percentage increase over the 2018 base salary of APPROXIMATELY
    A. 15%   B. 16%   C. 17%   D. 18%

11. If 17.5% of an employee's salary is withheld for taxes, the one of the following which is the fraction of the salary withheld is
    A. 3/20   B. 8/35   C. 7/40   D. 4/25

12. If a person withdraws 42% of the funds from his account with the retirement system, the remaining balance represents a fraction of MOST NEARLY
    A. 7/13   B. 5/9   C. 7/12   D. 4/7

13. A property decreases in value from $45,000 to $35,000. The percent of decrease is MOST NEARLY
    A. 20.5%   B. 22.2%   C. 25.0%   D. 28.6%

14. The fraction $\frac{487}{101326}$ expressed as a decimal is MOST NEARLY
    A. .0482   B. .00481   C. .0049   D. .00392

15. The reciprocal of the sum of 2/3 and 1/6 can be expressed as
    A. 0.83   B. 1.20   C. 1.25   D. 1.50

16. Total land and building costs for a new commercial property equal $50 per square foot.
    If the investors expect a 10 percent return on their costs, and if total operating expenses average 5 percent of total costs, annual gross rentals per square foot must be AT LEAST
    A. $7.50   B. $8.50   C. $10.00   D. $12.00

17. The formula for computing the amount of annual deposit in a compound interest bearing account to provide a lump sum at the end of a period of years is
    $X = \frac{r \cdot L}{(1+r)^{n-1}}$ (X is the amount of annual deposit, r is the rate of interest, and n is the number of years and L = lump sum).
    Using the formula, the annual amount of the deposit at the end of each year to accumulate $20,000 at the end of 3 years with interest at 2 percent on annual balances is
    A. $6,120.00   B. $6,203.33   C. $6,535.09   D. $6,666.66

18. An investor sold two properties at $150,000 each. On one he made a 2.5 percent profit. On the other, he suffered a 25 percent loss.
The NET result of his sales was
A. neither a gain nor a loss
B. a $20,000 loss
C. a $75,000 gain
D. a $75,000 loss

18.____

19. A contractor decides to install a chain fence covering the perimeter of a parcel 75 feet wide and 112 feet in depth.
Which one of the following represents the number of feet to be covered?
A. 187
B. 364
C. 374
D. 8,400

19.____

20. A builder estimates he can build an average of 4½ one-family homes to an acre. There are 640 acres to one square mile.
Which one of the following CORRECTLY represents the number of one-family homes the builder would estimate he can build on one square mile?
A. 1,280
B. 1,920
C. 2,560
D. 2,880

20.____

21. $.01059 deposit at 7 percent interest will yield $1.00 in 30 years.
If a person deposited $1,059 at 7 percent interest on April 4, 1991, which one of the following amounts would represent the worth of this deposit on March 31, 2021?
A. $100
B. $1,000
C. $10,000
D. $100,000

21.____

22. A building has an economic life of forty years.
Assuming the building depreciates at a constant annual rate, which one of the following CORRECTLY represents the yearly percentage of depreciation?
A. 2.0%
B. 2.5%
C. 5.0%
D. 7.0%

22.____

23. A building produces a gross income of $200,000 with a net income of $20,000, before mortgage charges and capital recapture. The owner is able to increase the gross income 5 percent without a corresponding increase in operating costs.
The effect upon the net income will be an INCREASE of
A. 5%
B. 10%
C. 12.5%
D. 50%

23.____

24. The present value of $1.00 not payable for 8 years, and at 10 percent interest, is $.4665.
Which of the following amounts represents the PRESENT value of $1,000 payable 8 years hence at 10 percent interest?
A. $46.65
B. $466.50
C. $4,665.00
D. $46,650.00

24.____

25. The amount of real property taxes to be levied by a city is $100 million. The assessment roll subject to taxation shows an assessed valuation of $2 billion. Which one of the following tax rates CORRECTLY represents the tax rate to be levied per $100 of assessed valuation?
A. $.50
B. $5.00
C. $50.00
D. $500.00

25.____

KEY (CORRECT ANSWERS)

1.	A		11.	C
2.	C		12.	C
3.	A		13.	B
4.	C		14.	B
5.	A		15.	B
6.	B		16.	A
7.	D		17.	C
8.	C		18.	B
9.	B		19.	C
10.	C		20.	D

21.	D
22.	B
23.	D
24.	B
25.	B

5 (#2)

SOLUTIONS TO PROBLEMS

1. $597.45 + $535.91 + $639.91 + $552.83 = $2,326.11. Then, $2,326.11 − (4)($525.50) = $224.11

2. Death benefit = ($13,486.50)$(\frac{3}{7})$ ≈ $5,779.92

3. $\frac{15}{28}$ ≈ 53.57%

4. $\frac{11}{12}$ ≈ 91.6% (closer to 91.7%)

5. $\frac{5}{12}$ ≈ 41.7%

6. ($4,725-$3,213) ÷ $4,725 = 32%

7. $\frac{28}{52}$ ≈ 54%

8. $\frac{16}{52}$ ≈ 30.7% (closer to 30.8%)

9. $\frac{2}{11}$ ≈ 18.2%

10. ($82,500 - $70,500) ÷ $70,500 = 17%

11. 17.5% = $\frac{175}{1000}$ = $\frac{7}{40}$

12. 100% - 42% = 58% = $\frac{58}{100}$ = $\frac{29}{50}$, closest to $\frac{7}{12}$ in selections

13. $\frac{\$10,000}{\$45,000}$ ≈ 22.2%

14. 487/101,216 ≈ .00481

15. $\frac{2}{3} + \frac{1}{6} = \frac{5}{6}$ Then, $1 \div \frac{5}{6} = \frac{6}{5}$ = 1.20

16. (.15)($50) = $7.50

17. x = (.02)($20,000)/[(1+.02)^3 − 1] = 400 ÷ .061208 ≈ $6,535.09

18. Sold 150,000, 25% loss = paid 200,000, loss of $50,000 Sold 150,000, 25% profit = paid 120,000, profit of 30,000 − 50,000 + 30,000 = 20,000 (loss)

19. Perimeter = (2)(75) + (2)(112) = 374 ft.

6 (#2)

20. (640)(4½) = 2,880 homes

21. (1÷.01059)(1059) = $100,000

22. 1÷4 = .025 = 2.5%

23. New gross income = ($200,000)(X1.05) = $210,000
    Then, ($210,000-$200,000) ÷ $20,000 = 50%

24. Let x = present value of $1,000. Then, $\frac{\$1.00}{\$.4665} = \frac{\$1000}{x}$
    Solving, x = $466.50

25. Let x = tax rate. Then, $\frac{\$100{,}000{,}000}{\$2{,}000{,}000{,}000} = \frac{x}{\$100}$
    Solving, x = $5.00

TEST 3

DIRECTIONS: Each question or incomplete statement is followed by several suggested answers or completions. Select the one that BEST answers the question or completes the statement. *PRINT THE LETTER OF THE CORRECT ANSWER IN THE SPACE AT THE RIGHT.*

1. It is found that for the past three years the average weekly number of inspections per inspector ranged from 20 inspections to 40 inspections.
   On the basis of this information, it is MOST reasonable to conclude that
   A. on the average, 30 inspections per week were made
   B. the average weekly number of inspections never fell below 20
   C. the performance of inspectors deteriorated over the three-year period
   D. the range in average weekly inspections was 60

1.____

Questions 2-4.

DIRECTIONS: Questions 2 through 4 are to be answered on the basis of the following information.

The number of students admitted to University X in 2019 from High School Y was 268 students. This represented 13.7 percent of University X's entering freshman classes. In 2020, it is expected that University X will admit 591 students from High School Y, which is expected to represent 19.4 percent of the 2020 entering freshman classes of University X.

2. Which of the following is CLOSEST estimate of the size of University's expected 2020 entering freshman classes?
   _____ students
   A. 2,000   B. 2,500   C. 3,000   D. 3,500

2.____

3. Of the following, the expected percentage of increase from 2019 to 2020 in the number of students graduating from High School Y and entering University X as freshmen is MOST NEARLY
   A. 5.7%   B. 20%   C. 45%   D. 120%

3.____

4. Assume that the cost of processing admission to University X from High School Y in 2019 was an average of $28. Also, that this was 1/3 more than the average cost of processing each of the other 2019 freshmen admissions to University X.
   Then, the one of the following that MOST closely shows the total processing cost of all 2019 freshman admissions to University X is
   A. $6,500   B. $20,000   C. $30,000   D. $40,000

4.____

5. Assume that during the fiscal year 2019-2020, a bureau produced 20% more work units than it produced in the fiscal year 2018-2019. Also assume that during the fiscal year 2019-2020 that bureau's staff was 20% smaller than it was in the fiscal year 2018-2019.

5.____

On the basis of this information, it would be MOST proper to conclude that the number of work units produced per staff member in that bureau in the fiscal year 2019-2020 exceeded the number of work units produced per staff member in that bureau in the fiscal year 2018-2019 by which one of the following percentages?
   A. 20%   B. 25%   C. 40%   D. 50%

6. Assume that during the following fiscal years (FY), a bureau has received the following appropriations:
    FY 2015-2016 - $200,000
    FY 2016-2017 - $240,000
    FY 2017-2018 - $280,000
    FY 2018-2019 - $390,000
    FY 2019-2020 - $505,000

   The bureau's appropriation for which one of the following fiscal years showed the LARGEST percentage of increase over the bureau's appropriation for the immediately previous fiscal year?
   A. FY 2016-2017   B. FY 2017-2018
   C. FY 2018-2019   D. FY 2010-2020

7. Assume that the number of buses (U_t) required for a given line-haul system serving the Central Business District depends upon roundtrip time (t), capacity of bus (c), and the total number of people to be moved in a peak hour (P) in the major direction, i.e., in the morning and out in the evening.
The formula for the number of buses required is U_t =
   A. Ptc   B. $\frac{tP}{c}$ C. $\frac{cP}{t}$ D. $\frac{ct}{P}$

8. The area, in blocks, that can be served by a single stop for any maximum walking distance is given by the following formula: $a = 2w^2$. In this formula, a = the area served by a stop and w = maximum walking distance.
If people will tolerate a walk of up to three blocks, how many stops would be needed to service an area of 288 square blocks?
   A. 9   B. 16   C. 18   D. 27

Questions 9-11.

DIRECTIONS: Questions 9 through 11 are to be answered on the basis of the following information.

In 2019, a police precinct records 456 cases of car thefts, which is 22.6 percent of all grand larcenies. In 2020, there were 560 such cases, which constituted 35% of the broader category.

9. The number of crimes in the broader category in 2020 was MOST NEARLY
   A. 1,600   B. 1,700   C. 1,960   D. 2,800

10. The change from 2019 to 2020 in the number of crimes in the broader category represented MOST NEARLY a
 A. 2.5% decrease
 B. 10.1% increase
 C. 12.5% increase
 D. 20% decrease

10.____

11. In 2020, one out of every 6 of these crimes was solved.
 This represents MOST NEARLY what percentage of the total number of crimes in the broader category that year?
 A. 5.8 B. 6 C. 9.3 D. 12

11.____

12. Assume that a maintenance shop does 5 brake jobs to every 3 front-end jobs. It does 8,000 jobs altogether in a 240-day year. In one day, one worker can do 3 front-end jobs or 4 brake jobs.
 About how many workers will be needed in the shop?
 A. 3 B. 5 C. 10 D. 18

12.____

13. Assume that the price of a certain item declines by 6% one year, and then increases by 5 and 10 percent, respectively, during the next two years.
 What is the OVERALL increase in price over the three-year period?
 A. 4.2 B. 6 C. 8.6 D. 10.1

13.____

14. After finding the total percent change in a price (TO) over a three-year period, as in the preceding question, one could compute the average annual percent change in the price by using the formula
 A. $(1+TC)^{1/3}$
 B. $\frac{(1+TC)}{3}$
 C. $(1+TC)^{1/3-1}$
 D. $\frac{1}{(1+TC)^{1/3}-1}$

14.____

15. 357 is 6% of
 A. 2,142 B. 5,950 C. 4,140 D. 5,900

15.____

16. In 2019, a department bought n pieces of a certain supply item for a total of $x. In 2020, the department bought k percent fewer of the item but had to pay a total of g percent more for it.
 Which of the following formulas is CORRECT for determining the average price per item in 2020?
 A. $100\frac{xg}{nk}$
 B. $\frac{x(100+g)}{n(100-k)}$
 C. $\frac{x(100-g)}{n(100+k)}$
 D. $\frac{x}{n} - 100\frac{g}{k}$

16.____

17. A sample of 18 income tax returns, each with 4 personal exemptions, is taken for 2019 and 2020. The breakdown is as follows in terms of income:

Average Gross Income (in thousands)	Number of Returns	
	2019	2020
40	6	2
80	10	11
120	2	5

There is a personal deduction per exemption of $500.
There are no other expense deductions. In addition, there is an exclusion of $3,000 for incomes less than $50,000 and $2,000 for incomes from $50,000 to $99,999.99. From $100,000 upward there is no exclusion.

17.____

The average net taxable income for the samples in thousands for 2019 is MOST NEARLY
   A. $67   B. $85   C. $10   D. $128

18. In the preceding question, the increase in average net taxable income for the sample (in thousands) between 2019 and 2020 is
    A. 16   B. 20   C. 24   D. 34

19. Assume that supervisor S has four subordinates—A, B, C, and D. The MAXIMUM number of relationships, assuming that all combinations are included, that can exist between S and his subordinates is
    A. 28   B. 15   C. 7   D. 4

20. If the workmen's compensation insurance rate for clerical workers is 93 cents per $100 of wages, the total premium paid by a city whose clerical staff earns $8,765,000 is MOST NEARLY
    A. $8,150   B. $81,515   C. $87,650   D. $93,765

21. Assume that a budget of $3,240,000,000 for the fiscal year beginning July 1, 2020 has been approved. A city sales tax is expected to provide $1,100,000,000; licenses, fees and sundry revenues ae expected to yield $121,600,000; the balance is to be raised from property taxes. A tax equalization board has appraised all property in the city at a fair value of $42,500,000,000. The council wishes to assess property at 60% of its fair value.
    The tax rate would need to be MOST NEARLY _____ per $100 of assessed value.
    A. $12.70   B. $10.65   C. $7.90   D. $4.00

22. Men's white linen handkerchiefs cost $12.90 for 3.
    The cost per dozen handkerchiefs is
    A. $77.40   B. $38.70   C. $144.80   D. $51.60

23. Assume that it is necessary to partition a room measuring 40 feet by 20 feet into eight smaller rooms of equal size.
    Allowing no room for aisles, the MINIMUM amount of partitioning that would be needed is _____ feet.
    A. 90   B. 100   C. 110   D. 140

24. Assume that two types of files have been ordered: 200 of type A and 100 of type B. When the files are delivered, the buyer discovers that 25% of each type is damaged. Of the remaining files, 20% of type A and 40% of type B are the wrong color.
    The total number of files that are the WRONG COLOR is
    A. 30   B. 40   C. 50   D. 60

25. In a unit of five inspectors, one inspector makes an average of 12 inspections a day, two inspectors make an average of 10 inspections a day, and two inspectors make an average of 9 inspections a day.
If in a certain week one of the inspectors who makes an average of nine inspections a day is out of work on Monday and Tuesday because of illness and all the inspectors do no inspections for half a day on Wednesday because of a special meeting, the number of inspections this unit can be expected to make in that week is MOST NEARLY

   A. 215   B. 225   C. 230   D. 250

25.____

KEY (CORRECT ANSWERS)

1.	B	11.	A
2.	C	12.	C
3.	D	13.	C
4.	D	14.	C
5.	D	15.	B
6.	C	16.	B
7.	B	17.	A
8.	B	18.	A
9.	A	19.	B
10.	D	20.	B

21. C
22. D
23. B
24. D
25. A

SOLUTIONS TO PROBLEMS

1. Since the number of weekly inspections ranged from 20 to 40, this implies that the average weekly number of inspections never fell below 20.

2. 591 ÷ 194 ≈ 3046, closest to 3,000 students

3. (591-268) ÷ 268 = 120%

4. Total processing cost = (268)(28) + (1,688)($21) = $42,952, closest to $40,000. [Note: Since 268 represents 13.7%, total freshman population = 268 ÷ .137 ≈ 1,956. Then, 1,956 − 268 = 1,688]

5. Let x = staff size in 2018-2019. Then, .80x = staff size in 2019-2020. Since the 2019-2020 staff produced 20% more work, this is represented by 1.20. However, to measure the productivity per staff member, the factor 1/.80 = 1.25 must also be used to equate the 2 staffs. Then, (1.20)(1.25) = 1.50. Thus, the 2019-2020 staff produced 50% more than the 2018-2019 staff.

6. The respective percent increases are ≈ 20%, 17%, 39%, 29%. The largest would be, over the previous fiscal year, for the current fiscal year 2018-2019

7. $\frac{P}{c}$ = number of buses needed per hour. If t = time (in hrs.), then U_t = tP.c

8. a = (2)(9) = 18 for 1 stop. Then, 288 ÷ 18 = 15 stops.

9. 560 ÷ .35 = 1600 grand larcenies.

10. 456 ÷ .226 = 2018; 560 ÷ .35 = 1600. Then, (1,600-2,018) ÷ 2,018 = -20% or a 20% decrease.

11. $(\frac{1}{6})(560) = 93\frac{1}{3}$. Then, $93\frac{1}{3}$ ÷ 1,600 = 5.8%

12. There are 5,000 brake jobs and 3,000 front-end jobs in one year.
5,000 ÷ 4 = 1,250 days, and 1,250 ÷ 240 ≈ 5.2. Also, 3,000 ÷ 3 = 1,000 days, and 1,000 ÷ 240 ≈ 4.2. Total number of workers needed ≈ 5.2 + 4.2 ≈ 10.

13. (.94)(1.05)(1.10) = 1.0857, which represents an overall increase by about 8.6%.

14. Average annual % change = $(1+TC)^{1/3} - 1 = (1.0857)^{1/3} - 1 ≈ 2.8\%$.

15. 357 ÷ .06 = 5,950

16. In 2020, $(h)(1-\frac{k}{100})$ pieces cost $(x)(1 + \frac{g}{100})$ dollars. To calculate the cost for 1 piece (average cost), find the value of $[(x)(1 + \frac{G}{100})] \div [(n)(1 - \frac{K}{100})] = [(x)(100+g)/100]$. $[100/\{n(100-k)\}] = [x(100+g)]/[n(100-k)]$

7 (#3)

17.

	#	Deductions Up to 50,000	
40,000	6	2000 3000	40,000−3,000−2,000 = 35,000 x 6
80,000	10	2000 2000	80,000−2,000−2,000 = 76,000 x 10
20,000	2	2000	= 118000 x 2

35,000 x 6 = 210,000 = 210
76,000 x 10 = 760,000 = 760
118,800 x 2 = 236,000 = 236
                                       1206

1206 ÷ 18 = 67

18. 2020   Deductions

40,000	2	2000 3000	35,000 x 2 =	70,000
80,000	11	2000 2000	76,000 x 11 =	836,000
120,000	5	2000	118,000 x 5 =	590,000
				1,496,000

1,496,000/18 = 83,111
83,111 − 67,000 = 16,111 = most nearly 16 (in thousands)

19. We are actually looking for the number of different groups of different sizes involving S. This reduces to $_4C_1 + {_4C_2} + {_4C_2} + {_4C_4}$ = 4 + 6 + 4 + 1 = 15. The notation $_nC_r$ means combinations of n things taken R at a time = $[(n)(n-1)(n-2)(...)(n-R+1)]/[(R)(R-1)(...)(1)]$. The 15 groups are: SA, SB, SC, SD, SAB, SAC, SAD, SBC, SBD, SCD, SABC, SABD, SACD, SBCD, SABCD.

20. Let x = total premiums. Then, $\frac{.93}{100} = \frac{X}{8,765,000}$ Solving, x = $81,515

21. The balance, raised from property taxes, = $3,240,000,000 - $1,100,000,000 − $121,600,000 = $2,018,400,000. Now, (.60)($42,500,000,000) = $25,500,000. The tax rate per $100 of assessed value = ($2,018,400,000)($100)(/$25,500,000,00 = $7.90.

22. A dozen costs ($12.90)($\frac{12}{3}$) = $51.60.

23. (40(20) ÷ 8 = 100 ft.

24. Total number of wrong-color files = (200)(.75)(.20)+(100)(.75)(.40) = 60

25. Weekly number of inspections = (12×5) + (10×5) + (10×5) + (9×5) + 9×5) = 250
Subtract: 9 Monday, 9 Tuesday, 25 Wednesday
Total: 250 − 9 − 9 − 25 = 207
Closest entry is choice A.

PREPARING WRITTEN MATERIAL

PARAGRAPH REARRANGEMENT
COMMENTARY

The sentences that follow are in scrambled order. You are to rearrange them in proper order and indicate the letter choice containing the correct answer at the space at the right.

Each group of sentences in this section is actually a paragraph presented in scrambled order. Each sentence in the group has a place in that paragraph; no sentence is to be left out. You are to read each group of sentences and decide upon the best order in which to put the sentences so as to form a well-organized paragraph.

The questions in this section measure the ability to solve a problem when all the facts relevant to its solution are not given.

More specifically, certain positions of responsibility and authority require the employee to discover connection between events sometimes, apparently, unrelated. In order to do this, the employee will find it necessary to correctly infer that unspecified events have probably occurred or are likely to occur. This ability becomes especially important when action must be taken on incomplete information.

Accordingly, these questions require competitors to choose among several suggested alternatives, each of which presents a different sequential arrangement of the events. Competitors must choose the MOST logical of the suggested sequences.

In order to do so, they may be required to draw on general knowledge to infer missing concepts or events that are essential to sequencing the given events. Competitors should be careful to infer only what is essential to the sequence. The plausibility of the wrong alternatives will always require the inclusion of unlikely events or of additional chains of events which are NOT essential to sequencing the given events.

It's very important to remember that you are looking for the best of the four possible choices, and that the best choice of all may not even be one of the answers you're given to choose from.

There is no one right way to solve these problems. Many people have found it helpful to first write out the order of the sentences, as they would have arranged them, on their scrap paper before looking at the possible answers. If their optimum answer is there, this can save them some time. If it isn't, this method can still give insight into solving the problem. Others find it most helpful to just go through each of the possible choices, contrasting each as they go along. You should use whatever method feels comfortable and works for you.

While most of these types of questions are not that difficult, we've added a higher percentage of the difficult type, just to give you more practice. Usually there are only one or two questions on this section that contain such subtle distinctions that you're unable to answer confidently. And you then may find yourself stuck deciding between two possible choices, neither of which you're sure about.

PREPARING WRITTEN MATERIAL
PARAGRAPH REARRANGEMENT
EXAMINATION SECTION
TEST 1

DIRECTIONS: The following groups of sentences need to be arranged in an order that makes sense. Select the letter preceding the sequence that represents the best sentence order. *PRINT THE LETTER OF THE CORRECT ANSWER IN THE SPACE AT THE RIGHT.*

1. I. The ostrich egg shell's legendary toughness makes it an excellent substitute for certain types of dishes or dinnerware, and in parts of Africa ostrich shells are cut and decorated for use as containers for water.
    II. Since prehistoric times, people have used the enormous egg of the ostrich as a part of their diet, a practice which has required much patience and hard work—to hard boil an ostrich egg takes about four hours.
    III. Opening the egg's shell, which is rock hard and nearly an inch thick, requires heavy tools, such as a saw or chisel; from inside, a baby ostrich must use a hornlike projection on its beak as a miniature pick-axe to escape from the egg.
    IV. The offspring of all higher-order animals originate from single egg cells that are carried by mothers, and most of these eggs are relatively small, often microscopic.
    V. The egg of the African ostrich, however, weighs a massive thirty pounds, making it the largest single cell on earth, and a common object of human curiosity and wonder.
    The BEST order is:
      A. V, IV, I, II, III   B. I, IV, V, III, II   C. IV, II, III, V, I   D. IV, V, II, III, I

1.____

2. I. Typically only a few feet high on the open sea, individual tsunami have been known to circle the entire globe two or three times if their progress is not interrupted, but are not usually dangerous until they approach the shallow water that surrounds land masses.
    II. Some of the most terrifying and damaging hazards caused by earthquakes are tsunami, which were once called "tidal waves"—a poorly chosen name, since these waves have nothing to do with tides.
    III. Then a wave, slowed by the sudden drag on the lower part of its moving water column, will pile upon itself, sometimes reaching a height of over 100 feet.
    IV. Tsunami (Japanese for "great harbor wave") are seismic waves that are caused by earthquakes near oceanic trenches, and once triggered, can travel up to 600 miles an hour on the open ocean.
    V. A land-shoaling tsunami is capable of extraordinary destruction; some tsunami have deposited large boats miles inland, washed out two-foot-thick seawalls, and scattered locomotive trains over long distances.
    The BEST order is:
      A. IV, I, III, II, V   B. I, III, IV, II, V   C. V, I, III, II, IV   D. II, IV, I, III, V

2.____

3. I. Soon, by the 1940s, jazz was the most popular type of music among American intellectuals and college students.
    II. In the early days of jazz, it was considered "lowdown" music, or music that was played only in rough, disreputable bars and taverns.
    III. However, jazz didn't take too long to develop from early ragtime melodies into more complex, sophisticated forms, such as Charlie Parker's "bebop" style of jazz.
    IV. After charismatic band leaders such as Duke Ellington and Count Basie brought jazz to a larger audience, and jazz continued to evolve into more complicated forms, white audiences began to accept and even to enjoy the new American art form.
    V. Many white Americans, who then dictated the tastes of society, were wary of music that was played almost exclusively in black clubs in the poorer sections of cities and towns.
    The BEST order is:
       A. V, IV, III, II, I   B. II, V, III, IV, I   C. IV, V, III, I, II   D. I, II, IV, III, V

3.____

4. I. Then, hanging in a windless place, the magnetized end of the needle would always point to the south.
    II. The needle could then be balanced on the rim of a cup, or the edge of a fingernail, but this balancing act was hard to maintain, and the needle often fell off.
    III. Other needles would point to the north, and it was important for any traveler finding his way with a compass to remember which kind of magnetized needle he was carrying.
    IV. To make some of the earliest compasses in recorded history, ancient Chinese "magicians" would rub a needle with a piece of magnetized iron called a lodestone.
    V. A more effective method of keeping the needle free to swing with its magnetic pull was to attach a strand of silk to the center of the needle with a tiny piece of wax.
    The BEST order is:
       A. IV, II, V, I, III   B. IV, III, V, II, I   C. IV, V, II, I, III   D. IV, I, III, V, II

4.____

5. I The now-famous first mate of the *H.M.S. Bounty*, Fletcher Christian, founded one of the world's most peculiar civilizations in 1790.
    II. The men knew they had just committed a crime for which they could be hanged, so they set sail for Pitcairn, a remote, abandoned island in the far eastern region of the Polynesian archipelago, accompanied by twelve Polynesian women and six men.
    III. In a mutiny that has become legendary, Christian and the others forced Captain Bligh into a lifeboat and set him adrift off the coast of Tonga in April of 1789.
    IV. In early 1790, the *Bounty* landed at Pitcairn Island, where the men lived out the rest of their lives and founded an isolated community which to this day includes direct descendants of Christian and the other Crewmen.

5.____

V. The *Bounty*, commanded by Captain William Bligh, was in the middle of a global voyage, and Christian and his shipmates had come to the conclusion that Bligh was a reckless madman who would lead them to their deaths unless they took the ship from him.

The BEST order is:
  A. IV, V, III, II, I   B. I, III, V, II, IV   C. I, V, III, II, IV   D. III, I, V, IV, II

6.
I. But once the vines had been led to make orchids, the flowers had to be carefully hand-pollinated, because unpollinated orchids usually lasted less than a day, wilting and dropping off the vine before it had even become dark.
II. The Totonac farmers discovered that looping a vine back around once it reached a five-foot height on its host tree would cause the vine to flower.
III. Though they knew how to process the fruit pods and extract vanilla's flavoring agent, the Totonacs also knew that a wild vanilla vine did not produce abundant flowers or fruit.
IV. Wild vines climbed along the trunks and canopies of trees, and this constant upward growth diverted most of the vine's energy to making leaves instead of the orchid flowers that once pollinated, would produce the flavorful pods.
V. Hundreds of years before vanilla became a prized food flavoring in Europe and the Western World, the Totonac Indians of the Mexican Gulf Coast were skilled cultivators of the vanilla vine, whose fruit they literally worshipped as a goddess.

The BEST order is:
  A. II, III, IV, I, V   B. II, IV, III, I, V   C. V, III, IV, II, I   D. III, IV, I, II, V

6._____

7.
I. Once airborne, the spider is at the mercy of the air currents—usually the spider takes a brief journey, traveling close to the ground, but some have been found in air samples collected as high as 10,000 feet, or been reported landing on ships far out at sea.
II. Once a young spider has hatched, it must leave the environment into which it was born as quickly as possible, in order to avoid competing with its hundreds of brothers and sisters for food.
III. The silk rises into warm air currents, and as soon as the pull feels adequate the spider lets go and drifts up into the air, suspended from the silk strand in the same way that a person might parasail.
IV. To help young spiders do this, many species have adapted a practice known as "aerial dispersal," or, in common speech, "ballooning."
V. A spider that wants to leave its surroundings quickly will climb to the top of a grass system or twig, face into the wind, and aim its back end into the air, releasing a long stream of silk from the glands near the tip of its abdomen.

The BEST order is:
  A. V, IV, II, III, I   B. V, II, IV, I, III   C. II, V, IV, III, I   D. II, IV, V, III, I

7._____

8. I. For about a year, Tycho worked at a castle in Prague with a scientist named Johannes Kepler, but their association was cut short by another argument that drove Kepler out of the castle, to later develop, on his own, the theory of planetary orbits.
    II. Tycho found life without a nose embarrassing, so he made a new nose for himself out of silver, which reportedly remained glued to his face for the rest of his life.
    III. Tycho Brahe, the 17th-century Danish astronomer, is today more famous for his odd and arrogant personality than for any contribution he has made to our knowledge of the stars and planets.
    IV. Early in his career, as a student at Rostock University, Tycho got into an argument with another student about who was the better mathematician, and the two became so angry that the argument turned into a sword fight, during which Tycho's nose was sliced off.
    V. Later in his life, Tycho's arrogance may have kept him from playing a part in one of the greatest astronomical discoveries in history: the elliptical orbits of the solar system's planets.

    The BEST order is:
    A. I, IV, II, III, V   B. IV, II, III, V, I   C. IV, II, I, III, V   D. III, IV, II, V, I

9. I. The processionaries are so used to this routine that if a person picks up the end of a silk line and brings it back to the origin—creating a closed circle—the caterpillars may travel around and around for days, sometimes starving or freezing, without changing course.
    II. Rather than relying on sight or sound, the other caterpillars, who are lined up end-to-end behind the leader, travel to and from their nests by walking on this silk line, and each will reinforce it by laying down its own marking line as it passes over.
    III. In order to insure the safety of individuals, the processionary caterpillar nests in a tree with dozens of other caterpillars, and at night, when it is safest, they all leave together in search of food.
    IV. The processionary caterpillar of the European continent is a perfect illustration of how much some inspect species rely on instinct in their daily routines.
    V. As they leave their nests, the processionaries form a single-file line behind a leader who spins and lays out a silk line to mark the chosen path.

    The BEST order is:
    A. IV, III, V, II, I   B. III, V, IV, II, I   C. III, V, II, I, IV   D. IV, V, III, I, II

10. I. Often, the child is also given a handcrafted walker or push cart, to provide support for its first upright explorations.
    II. In traditional Indian families, a child's first steps are celebrated as a ceremonial event, rooted in ancient myth.
    III. These carts are often intricately designed to resemble the chariot of Krishna, an important figure in Indian mythology.
    IV. The sound of these anklet bells is intended to mimic the footsteps of the legendary child Rama, who is celebrated in devotional songs throughout India.

V. When the child's parents see that the child is ready to begin walking, they will fit it with specially designed ankle bracelets, adorned with gently ringing bells.

The BEST order is:
A. II, III, IV, I, V   B. II, V, III, I, IV   C. V, IV, I, III, II   D. V, III, II, I, IV

11. I. The settlers planted Osage oranges all across Middle America, and today long lines and rectangles of Osage orange trees can still be seen on the prairies, running along the former boundaries of farms that no longer exist.
   II. After trying sod walls and water-filled ditches with no success, American farmers began to look for a plant that was adaptable to prairie weather, and that could be trimmed into a hedge that was "pig-tight, horse-high, and bull-strong."
   III. The tree, so named because it bore a large (but inedible) fruit the size of an orange, was among the sturdiest and hardiest of American trees, and was prized among Native Americans for the strength and flexibility of bows which were made from its wood.
   IV. The first people to practice agriculture on the American flatlands were faced with an important problem: what would they use to fence their land in a place that was almost entirely without trees or rocks?
   V. Finally, an Illinois farmer brought the settlers a tree that was native to the land between the Red and Arkansas rivers, a tree called the Osage orange.

The BEST order is:
A. II, I, V, III, IV   B. I, II, III, IV, V   C. IV, II, V, III, I   D. IV, II, I, III, V

12. I. After about ten minutes of such spirited and complicated activity, the head dancer is free to make up his or her own movements while maintaining the interest of the New Year's crowd.
   II. The dancer will then perform a series of leg kicks, while at the same time operating the lion's mouth with his own hand and moving the ears and eyes by means of a string which is attached to the dancer's own mouth.
   III. The most difficult role of this dance belongs to the one who controls the lion's head; this person must lead all the other "parts" of the lion through the choreographed segments of the dance.
   IV. The head dancer begins with a complex series of steps. alternately stepping forward with the head raised, and then retreating a few steps while lowering the head, a movement that is intended to create the impression that the lion is keeping a watchful eye for anything evil.
   V. When performing a traditional Chinese New Year's lion dance, several performers must fit themselves inside a large lion costume and work together to enact different parts of the dance.

The BEST order is:
A. V, III, IV, II, I   B. III, IV, II, V, I   C. III, I, V, IV, II   D. IV, II, III, V, I

13.
   I. For many years the shell of the chambered nautilus was treasured in Europe for its beauty and intricacy, but collectors were unaware that they were in possession of the structure that marked a "missing link" in the evolution of marine mollusks.
   II. The nautilus, however, evolved a series of enclosed chambers in its shell, and invented a new use for the structure: the shell began to serve as a buoyancy device.
   III. Equipped with this new flotation device, the nautilus did not need the single, muscular foot of its predecessors, but instead developed flaps, tentacles, and a gentle form of jet propulsion that transformed it into the first mollusk able to take command of its own density and explore a three-dimensional world.
   IV. By pumping and adjusting air pressure into the chambers, the nautilus could spend the day resting on the bottom, and then rise toward the surface at night in search of food.
   V. The nautilus shell looks like a large snail shell, similar to those of its ancestors, who used their shells as protective coverings while they were anchored to the sea floor.
   The BEST order is:
   A. V, II, IV, I, III   B. V, I, II, III, IV   C. I, II, V, III, IV   D. I, V, II, IV, III

14.
   I. While France and England battled for control of the region, the Acadiens prospered on the fertile farmland, which was finally secured by England in 1713.
   II. Early in the 17th century, settlers from Western France founded a colony called Acadie in what is now the Canadian province of Nova Scotia.
   III. At this time, English officials feared the presence of spies among the Acadiens who might be loyal to their French homeland, and the Acadiens were deported to spots along the Atlantic and Caribbean shores of America.
   IV. The French settlers remained on this land, under English rule, for around forty years, until the beginning of the French and Indian War, another conflict between France and England.
   V. As the Acadien refugees drifted toward a final home in Southern Louisiana, neighbors shortened their name to "Cadien," and finally "Cajun," the name which the descendants of early Acadiens still call themselves.
   The BEST order is:
   A. I, IV, II, III, V   B. II, I, III, V, IV   C. II, I, IV, III, V   D. V, II, III, IV, I

15.
   I. Traditional households in the Eastern and Western regions of Africa serve two meals a day—one at around noon, and the other in the evening.
   II. The starch is then used in the way that Americans might use a spoon, to scoop up a portion of the main dish on the person's plate.
   III. The reason for the starch's inclusion in every meal has to do with taste as well as nutrition; African food can be very spicy, and the starch is known to cool the burning effect of the main dish.
   IV. When serving these meals, the main dish is usually served on individual plates, and the starch is served on a communal plate, from which diners break off a piece of bread or scoop rice or fufu in their fingers.

V. The typical meals usually consist of a thick stew or soup as the main course, and an accompanying starch—either bread, rice, or *fufu*, a starchy grain paste similar in consistency to mashed potatoes.

The BEST order is:
A. V, II, III, IV, I B. V, I, IV, III, II C. I, IV, V, III, II D. I, V, IV, II, III

16.
I. In the early days of the American Midwest, Indiana settlers sometimes came together to hold an event called an apple peeling, where neighboring settlers gathered at the homestead of a host family to help prepare the hosts' apple crop for cooking, canning, and making apple butter.
II. At the beginning of the event, each peeler sat down in front of a ten- or twenty-gallon stone jar and was given a crock of apples and a paring knife.
III. Once a peeler had finished with a crock, another was placed next to him; if the peeler was an unmarried man, he kept a strict count of the number of apples he had peeled, because the winner was allowed to kiss the girl of his choice.
IV. The peeling usually ended by 9:30 in the evening, when the neighbors gathered in the host family's parlor for a dance social.
V. The apples were peeled, cored, and quartered, and then placed into the jar.

The BEST order is:
A. I, V, III, IV, II B. II, V, III, IV, I C. I, II, V, III, IV D. II, I, V, IV, III

16.____

17.
I. If your pet turtle is a land turtle and is native to temperate climates, it will stop eating some time in October, which should be your cue to prepare the turtle for hibernation.
II. The box should then be covered with a wire screen, which will protect the turtle from any rodents or predators that might want to take advantage of a motionless and helpless animal.
III. When your turtle hasn't eaten for a while and appears ready to hibernate, it should be moved to its winter quarters, most likely a cellar or garage, where the temperature should range between 40° and 45°F.
IV. Instead of feeding the turtle, you should bathe it every day in warm water, to encourage the turtle to empty its intestines in preparation for its long winter sleep.
V. Here the turtle should be placed in a well-ventilated box whose bottom is covered with a moisture-absorbing layer of clay beads, and then filled three-fourths full with almost dry peat moss or wood chips, into which the turtle will burrow and sleep for several months.

The BEST order is:
A. I, IV, III, V, II B. III, IV, II, V, I C. III, II, IV, I, V D. IV, V, II, III, I

17.____

18.
I. Once he has reached the nest, the hunter uses two sturdy bamboo poles like huge chopsticks to pull the next away from the mountainside, into a large basket that will be lowered to people waiting below.
II. The world's largest honeybees colonize the Nealese mountainsides, building honeycombs as large as a person on sheer rock faces that are often hundreds of feet high.

18.____

III. In the remote mountain country of Nepal, a small band of "honey hunters" carry out a tradition so ancient that 10,000 year-old drawings of the practice have been found in the caves of Nepal.
IV. To harvest the honey and beeswax from these combs, a honey hunter climbs above the nests, lowers a long bamboo-fiber ladder over the cliff, and then climbs down.
V. Throughout this dangerous practice, the hunter is stung repeatedly, and only the veterans, with skin that has been toughened over the years, are able to return from a hunt without the painful swelling caused by stings.

The BEST order is:
A. II, IV, III, V, I   B. II, IV, I, V, III   C. V, III, II, IV, I   D. III, II, IV, I, V

19. I. After the Romans left Britain, there were relentless attacks on the islands from the barbarian tribes of northern Germany—the Angles, Saxons, and Jutes.
II. As the empire weakened, Roman soldiers withdrew from Britain, leaving behind a country that continued to practice the Christian religion that had been introduced by the Romans.
III. Early Latin writings tell of a Christian warrior named Arturius (Arthur, in English) who led the British citizens to defeat these barbarian invades, and brought an extended period of peace to the lands of Britain.
IV. Long ago, the British Isles were part of the far-flung Roman Empire that extended across most of Europe and into Africa and Asia.
V. The romantic legend of King Arthur and his knights of the Round Table, one of the most popular and widespread stories of all time, appears to have some foundation in history.

The BEST order is:
A. V, IV, III, II, I   B. V, IV, II, I, III   C. IV, V, II, III, I   D. IV, III, II, I, V

19.____

20. I. The cylinder was allowed to cool until it could stand on its own, and then it was cut from the tube and split down the side with a single straight cut.
II. Nineteenth-century glassmakers, who had not yet discovered the glazier's modern techniques for making panes of glass, had to create a method for converting their blown gas into flat sheets.
III. The bubble was then pierced at the end to make a hole that opened up while the glassmaker gently spun it, creating a cylinder of glass.
IV. Turned on its side and laid on a conveyor belt, the cylinder was strengthened, or tempered, by being heated again and cooled very slowly, eventually flattening out into a single rectangular of glass.
V. To do this, the glassmaker dipped the end of a long tube into melted glass and blew into the other end of the tube, creating an expanding bubble of glass.

The BEST order is:
A. II, V, III, IV, I   B. II, IV, V, III, I   C. III, V, II, IV, I   D. III, I, IV, V, II

20.____

21. I. The splints are almost always hidden, but horses are occasionally born whose splinted toes project from the leg on either side, just above the hoof.
    II. The second and fourth toes remained, but shrank to thin splints of bone that fused invisibly to the horse's leg bone.
    III. Horses are unique among mammals, having evolved feet that each end in what is essentially a single toe, capped by a large, sturdy hoof.
    IV. Julius Caesar, an emperor of ancient Rome, was said to have owned one of these three-toed horses, and considered it so special that he would not permit anyone else to ride it.
    V. Though the horse's earlier ancestors possessed the traditional mammalian set of five toes on each foot, the horse has retained only its third toe; its first and fifth toes disappeared completely as the horse evolved.
    The BEST order is:
     A. III, V, II, I, IV   B. V, III, II, IV, I   C. III, II, V, I, IV   D. V, II, III, I, IV

22. I. The new building materials—some of which are twenty feet long, and weigh nearly six tons—were transported to Pohnpei on rafts, and were brought into their present position by using hibiscus fiber ropes and leverage to move the stone columns upward along the inclined trunks of coconut palm trees.
    II. The ancestors built great fires to heat the stone, and then poured cool seawater on the columns, which caused the stone to contract and split along natural fracture lines.
    III. The now-abandoned enclave of Nan Madol, a group of 92 man-made islands off the shore of the Micronesian island of Pohnpei, is estimated to have been built around the year 500 A.D.
    IV. The islanders say their ancestors quarried stone columns from a nearby island, where large basalt columns were formed by the cooling of molten lava.
    V. The structures of Nan Madol are remarkable for the sheer size of some of the stone "longs" or columns that were used to create the walls of the offshore community, and today anthropologists can only rely on the information of existing local people for clues about how Nan Madol was built.
    The BEST order is:
     A. V, IV, III, II, I   B. V, III, I, IV, II   C. III, V, IV, II, I   D. III, I, IV, II, V

23. I. One of the most easily manipulated substances on earth, glass can be made into ceramic tiles that are composed of over 90% air.
    II. NASA's space shuttles are the first spacecraft ever designed to leave and re-enter the earth's atmosphere while remaining intact.
    III. These ceramic tiles are such effective insulators that when a tile emerges from the oven in which it was fired, it can be held safely in a person's hand by the edges while its interior still glows at a temperature well over 2000°F.
    IV. Eventually, the engineers were led to a material that is as old as our most ancient civilization.
    V. Because the temperature during atmospheric re-entry is so incredibly hot, it took NASA's engineers some time to find a substance capable of protecting the shuttles.

The BEST order is:
A. V, II, I, II, IV   B. II, V, IV, I, III   C. II, III, I, IV, V   D. V, IV, III, I, II

24. I. The secret to teaching any parakeet to talk is patience, and the understanding that when a bird talks," it is simply imitating what it hears, rather than putting ideas into words.
    II. You should stay just out of sight of the bird and repeat the phrase you want it to learn, for at least fifteen minutes every morning and evening.
    III. It is important to leave the bird without any words of encouragement or farewell; otherwise it might combine stray remarks or phrases, such as "Good night," with the phrase you are trying to teach it.
    IV. For this reason, to train your bird to imitate your words you should keep it free of any distractions, especially other noises, while you are giving it "lesson."
    V. After your repetition, you should quietly leave the bird alone for a while, to think over what it has just heard.
    The BEST order is:
    A. I, IV, II, V, III   B. I, II, IV, III, V   C. III, II, I, V, IV   D. III, I, V, IV, II

24.____

25. I. As a school approaches, fishermen from neighboring communities join their fishing boats together as a fleet, and string their gill nets together to make a huge fence that is held up by cork floats.
    II. At a signal from the party leaders, or *nakura*, the family members pound the sides of the boats or beat the water with long poles, creating a sudden and deafening noise.
    III. The fishermen work together to drag the trap into a half-circle that may reach 300 yards in diameter, and then the families move their boats to form the other half of the circle around the school of fish.
    IV. The school of fish flee from the commotion into the awaiting trap, where a final wall of net is thrown over the open end of the half-circle, securing the day's haul.
    V. Indonesian people from the area around the Sulu islands live on the sea, in floating villages made of lashed-together or stilted homes, and make much of their living by fishing their home waters for migrating schools of snapper, scad, and other fish.
    The BEST order is:
    A. I, V, III, IV, II   B. I, II, IV, III, V   C. V, I, II, III, IV   D. V, I, III, II, IV

25.____

KEY (CORRECT ANSWERS)

1.	D	11.	C
2.	D	12.	A
3.	B	13.	D
4.	A	14.	C
5.	C	15.	D
6.	C	16.	C
7.	D	17.	A
8.	D	18.	D
9.	A	19.	B
10.	B	20.	A

21. A
22. C
23. B
24. A
25. D

PREPARING WRITTEN MATERIAL
EXAMINATION SECTION
TEST 1

DIRECTIONS: The following groups of sentences need to be arranged in an order that makes sense. Select the letter preceding the sequence that represents the BEST sentence order. *PRINT THE LETTER OF THE CORRECT ANSWER IN THE SPACE AT THE RIGHT.*

1. I. A large Naval station on Alameda Island, near Oakland, held many warships in port, and the War Department was worried that if the bridge were to be blown up by the enemy, passage to and from the bay would be hopelessly blocked.
    II. Though many skeptics were opposed to the idea of building such an enormous bridge, the most vocal opposition came from a surprising source: the United States War Department.
    III. The War Department's concerns led to a showdown at San Francisco City Hall between Strauss and the Secretary of War, who demanded to know what would happen if a military enemy blew up the bridge.
    IV. In 1933, by submitting a construction cost estimate of $17 million, an engineer named Joseph Strauss won the contract to build the Golden Gate Bridge of San Francisco, which would then become one of the world's largest bridges.
    V. Strauss quickly ended the debate by explaining that the Golden Gate Bridge was to be a suspension bridge, whose roadway would hang in the air from cables strung between two huge towers, and would immediately sink into three hundred feet of water if it were destroyed.
    The BEST order is:
    A. II, III, I, IV, V   B. I, II, III, V, IV   C. IV, II, I, III, V   D. IV, I, III, V, II

1.____

2. I. Plastic surgeons have already begun to use virtual reality to map out the complex nerve and tissue structures of a particular patient's face, in order to prepare for delicate surgery.
    II. A virtual reality program responds to these movements by adjusting the images that a person sees on a screen or through goggles, thereby creating an "interactive" world in which a person can see and touch three-dimensional graphic objects.
    III. No more than a computer program that is designed to build and display graphic images, the virtual reality program takes graphic programs a step further by sensing a person's head and body movements.
    IV. The computer technology known as virtual reality, now in its very first stages of development, is already revolutionizing some aspects of contemporary life.
    V. Virtual reality computers are also being used by the space program, most recently to simulate conditions for the astronauts who were launched on a repair mission to the Hubble telescope.

2.____

The BEST order is:
A. IV, II, I, V, III B. III, I, V, II, IV C. IV, III, II, I, V D. III, I, II, IV, V

3. I. Before you plant anything, the soil in your plant bed should be carefully raked level, a small section at a time, and any clods or rocks that can't be broken up should be removed.
   II. Your plant should be placed in a hole that will position it at the same level it was at the nursery, and a small indentation should be pressed into the soil around the plant in order to hold water near its roots.
   III. Before placing the plant in the soil, lightly separate any roots that may have been matted together in the container, cutting away any thick masses that can't be separated, so that the remaining roots will be able to grow outward.
   IV. After the bed is ready, remove your plant from its container by turning it upside down and tapping or pushing on the bottom —never remove it by pulling on the plant.
   V. When you bring home a small plant in an individual container from the nursery, there are several things to remember while preparing to plant it in your own garden.
   The BEST order is:
   A. V, IV, III, II, I B. V, II, IV, III, II C. I, IV, II, III, V D. I, IV, V, II, III

4. I. The motte and its tower were usually built first, so that sentries could use it as a lookout to warn the castle workers of any danger that might approach the castle.
   II. Though the moat and palisade offered the bailey a good deal of protection, it was linked to the motte by a set of stairs that led to a retractable drawbridge at the motte's gate, to enable people to evacuate onto the motte in case of an attack.
   III. The motte of these early castles was a fortified hill, sometimes as high as one hundred feet, on which stood a palisade and tower.
   IV. The bailey was a clear, level spot below the motte, also enclosed by a palisade, which in turn was surrounded by a large trench or moat.
   V. The earliest castles built in Europe were not the magnificent stone giants that still tower over much of the European landscape, but simpler wooden constructions called motte-and-bailey castles.
   The BEST order is:
   A. V, III, I, IV, II B. V, IV, I, II, III C. I, IV, III, II, V D. I, III, II, IV, V

5. I. If an infant is left alone or abandoned for a short while, its immediate response is to cry loudly, accompanying its screams with aggressive flailing of its legs and limbs.
   II. If a child has been abandoned for a longer period of time, it becomes completely still and quiet, as if realizing that now its only chance for survival is to shut its mouth and remain motionless.
   III. Along with their intense fear of the dark, the crying behavior of human infants offers insights into how prehistoric newborn children might have evolved instincts that would prevent them from becoming victims of predators.

IV. This behavior often surprises people who enter a hospital's maternity ward for the first time and encounter total silence from a roomful of infants.
V. This violent screaming response is quite different from an infant's cries of discomfort or hunger, and seems to serve as either the child's first line of defense against an unwanted intruder, or a desperate attempt to communicate its position to the mother.

The BEST order is:
A. III, II, IV, I, V B. III, I, V, II, IV C. I, V, IV, II, III D. II, IV, I, V, III

6.
I. When two cats meet who are strangers, their first actions and gestures determine who the "dominant" cat will be, at least for the time being.
II. Unlike dogs, cats are typically a solitary animal species who avoid social interaction, but they do display specific social responses to each other upon meeting.
III. This is unlikely, however; before such a point of open hostility is reached, one of the cats will usually take the "submissive" position of crouching down while looking away from the other dat.
IV. If a cat desires dominance or sees the other cat as a threat to its territory, it will stare directly at the intruder with a lowered tail.
V. If the other cat responds with a similar gesture, or with the strong defensive posture of an arched back, laid-back ears and raised tail, a fight or chase is likely if neither cat gives in.

The BEST order is:
A. IV, II, I, V, III B. I, II, IV, V, III C. I, IV, V, III, II D. II, I, IV, V, III

7.
I. A star or planet's gravitational force can best be explained in this way: anything passing through this "dent" in space will veer toward the star or planet as if it were rolling into a hole.
II. Objects that are massive or heavy, such as stars or planets, "sink" into this surface, creating a sort of dent or concavity in the surrounding space.
III. Black holes, the most massive objects known to exist in space, create dents so large and deep that the space surrounding them actually folds in on itself, preventing anything that falls in —even light —from ever escaping again.
IV. The sort of dent a star or planet makes depends on how massive it is; planets generally have weak gravitational pulls, but stars, which are larger and heavier, make a bigger "dent" that will attract more matter.
V. In outer space, the force of gravity works as if the surrounding space is a soft, flat surface.

The BEST order is:
A. III, V, II, I, IV B. III, IV, I, V, II C. V, II, I, IV, III D. I, V, II, IV, III

8.
I. Eventually, the society of Kyoto gave the world one of its first and greatest novels when Japan's most promising writer, Lady Murasaki Shikibu, wrote her chronicle of Kyoto's society, *The Tale of Genji*, which preceded the first European novels by more than 500 years.
II. The society of Kyoto was dedicated to the pleasures of art; the courtiers experimented with new and colorful methods of sculpture, painting, writing, decorative gardening, and even making clothes.

III. Japanese culture began under the powerful authority of Chinese Buddhism, which influenced every aspect of Japanese life from religion to politics and art.
IV. This new, vibrant culture was so sophisticated that all the people in Kyoto's imperial court considered themselves poets, and the line between life and art hardly existed —lovers corresponded entirely through written verses, and even government officials communicated by writing poems to each other.
V. In the eighth century, when the emperor established the town of Kyoto as the capital of the Japanese empire, Japanese society began to develop its own distinctive style.

The BEST order is:
A. V, II, IV, I, III   B. II, I, V, IV, III   C. V, III, IV, I, II   D. III, V, II, IV, I

9. I. Instead of wheels, the HSST uses two sets of magnets, one which sits on the track, and another that is carried by the train; these magnets generate an identical magnetic field which forces the two sets apart.
    II. In the last few decades, railway travel has become less popular throughout the world, because it is much slower than travel by airplane, and not much less expensive.
    III. The HSST's designers say that the train can take passengers from one town to another as quickly as a jet plane —while consuming less than half the energy.
    IV. This repellent effect is strong enough to lift the entire train above the trackway, and the train, literally traveling on air, rockets along at speeds of up to 300 miles per hour.
    V. The revolutionary technology of magnetic levitation, currently being tested by Japan's experimental HSST (High Speed Surface Transport), may yet bring passenger trains back from the dead.

    The BEST order is:
    A. II, V, I, IV, III   B. II, I, IV, III, V   C. V, II, III, I, IV   D. V, I, III, IV, II

10. I. When European countries first began to colonize the African continent, their impression of the African people was of a vast group of loosely organized tribal societies, without any great centralized source of power or wealth.
    II. The legend of Timbuktu persisted until the nineteenth century, when a French adventurer visited Timbuktu and found that raids by neighboring tribesmen had made the city a shadow of its former self.
    III. In the fifteenth century, when the stories of travelers who had traveled Africa's Sudan region began circulating around Europe, this impression began to change.
    IV. In 1470, an Italian merchant named Benedetto Dei traveled to Timbuktu and confirmed these rumors, describing a thriving metropolis where rich and poor people worshipped together in the city's many ornate mosques — there was even a university in Timbuktu, much like its European counterparts, where African scholars pursued their studies in the arts and sciences.

V. The travelers' legends told of an enormous city in the western Sudan, Timbuktu, where the streets were crowded with goods brought by faraway caravans, and where there was a stone palace as large as any in Europe.

The BEST order is:

A. III, V, I, IV, II   B. I, II, IV, III, V   C. I, III, V, IV, II   D. II, I, III, IV, V

11.
I. Also, our reference points in sighting the moon make us believe that its size is changing; when the moon is rising through the trees, it seems huge, because our brains unconsciously compare the size of the moon with the size of the trees in the foreground.
II. To most people, the sky itself appears more distant at the horizon than directly overhead, and if the moon's size—which remains constant—is projected from the horizon, the apparent distance of the horizon makes the moon look bigger.
III. Up higher in the sky, the moon is set against tiny stars in the background, which will make the moon seem smaller.
IV. People often wonder why the moon becomes bigger when it approaches the horizon, but most scientists agree that this is a complicated optical illusion, produced by at least three factors.
V. The moon illusion may also be partially explained by a phenomenon that has nothing to do with errors in our perception—light that enters the earth's atmosphere is sometimes refracted, and so the atmosphere may act as a kind of magnifying glass for the moon's image.

The BEST order is:

A. IV, III, V, II, I   B. IV, II, I, III, V   C. V, II, I, III, IV   D. II, I, III, IV, V

12.
I. When the Native Americans were introduced to the horses used by white explorers, they were amazed at their new alternative—here was an animal that was strong and swift, would patiently carry a person or other loads on its back, and they later discovered, was right at home on the plains.
II. Before the arrival of European explorers to North America, the natives of the American plains used large dogs to carry their travois-long lodgepoles loaded with clothing, gear, and food.
III. These horses, it is now known, were not really strangers to North America; the very first horses originated here, on this continent, tens of thousands of years ago, and migrated into Asia across the Bering Land Bridge, a strip of land that used to link our continent with the Eastern world.
IV. At first, the natives knew so little about horses that at least one tribe tried to feed their new animals pieces of dried meat and animal fat, and were surprised when the horses turned their heads away and began to eat the grass of the prairie.
V. The American horse eventually became extinct, but its Asian cousins were reintroduced to the New World when the European explorers brought them to live among the Native Americans.

The BEST order is:

A. II, I, IV, III, V   B. II, IV, I, III, V   C. I, II, IV, III, V   D. I, III, V, II, IV

13.
  I. The dress worn by the dancer is believed to have been adorned in the past by shells which would strike each other as the dancer performed, creating a lovely sound.
  II. Today's jingle-dress is decorated with the tin lids of snuff cans, which are rolled into cones and sewn onto the dress,
  III. During the jingle-dress dance, the dancer must blend complicated footwork with a series of gentle hos that cause the cones to jingle in rhythm to a drumbeat.
  IV. When contemporary Native American tribes meet for a pow-wow, one of the most popular ceremonies to take place is the women's jingle-dress dance.
  V. Besides being more readily available than shells, the lids are thought by many dancers to create a softer, more subtle sound.
  The BEST order is:
  A. II, IV, V, I, III   B. IV, II, I, III, V   C. II, I, III, V, IV   D. IV, I, II, V, III

14.
  I. If a homeowner lives where seasonal climates are extreme, deciduous shade trees—which will drop their leaves in the winter and allow sunlight to pass through the windows—should be planted near the southern exposure in order to keep the house cool during the summer.
  II. This trajectory is shorter and lower in the sky than at any other time of year during the winter, when a house most requires heating; the northern-facing parts of a house do not receive any direct sunlight at all.
  III. In designing an energy-efficient house, especially in colder climates, it is important to remember that most of the house's windows should face south.
  IV. Though the sun always rises in the east and sets in the west, the sun of the northern hemisphere is permanently situated in the southern portion of the sky.
  V. The explanation for why so many architects and builders want this "southern exposure" is related to the path of the sun in the sky.
  The BEST order is:
  A. III, I, V, IV, II   B. III, V, IV, II, I   C. I, III, IV, II, V   D. I, II, V, IV, III

15.
  I. His journeying lasted twenty-four years and took him over an estimated 75,000 miles, a distance that would not be surpassed by anyone other than Magellan—who sailed around the world—for another six hundred years.
  II. Perhaps the most far-flung of these lesser-known travelers was Ibn Batuta, an African Moslem who left his birthplace of Tangier in the summer of 1325.
  III. Ibn Batuta traveled all over Africa and Asia, from Niger to Peking, and to the islands of Maldive and Indonesia.
  IV. However, a few explorers of the Eastern world logged enough miles and adventures to make Marco Polo's voyage look like an evening stroll.
  V. In America, the most well-known of the Old World's explorers are usually Europeans such as Marco Polo, the Italian who brought many elements of Chinese culture to the Western world.
  The BEST order is:
  A. V, IV, II, III, I   B. V, IV, III, II, I   C. III, II, I, IV, V   D. II, III, I, IV, V

16.
   I. In the rainforests of South America, a rare species of frog practices a reproductive method that is entirely different from this standard process.
   II. She will eventually carry each of the tadpoles up into the canopy and drop each into its own little pool, where it will be easy to locate and safe from most predators.
   III. After fertilization, the female of the species, who lives almost entirely on the forest floor, lays between 2 and 16 eggs among the leaf litter at the base of a tree, and stands watch over these eggs until they hatch.
   IV. Most frogs are pond-dwellers who are able to deposit hundreds of eggs in the water and then leave them alone, knowing that enough eggs have been laid to insure the survival of some of their offspring.
   V. Once the tadpoles emerge, the female backs in among them, and a tadpole will wriggle onto her back to be carried high into the forest canopy, where the female will deposit it in a little pool of water cupped in the leaf of a plant.
   The BEST order is:
   A. I, IV, III, II, V   B. I, III, V, II, IV   C. IV, III, II, V, I   D. IV, I, III, V, II

16.____

17.
   I. Eratosthenes had heard from travelers that at exactly noon on June 21, in the ancient city of Aswan, Egypt, the sun cast no shadow in a well, which meant that the sun must be directly overhead.
   II. He knew the sun always cast a shadow in Alexandria, and so he figured that if he could measure the length of an Alexandria shadow at the time when there was no shadow in Aswan, he could calculate the angle of the sun, and therefore the circumference of the earth.
   III. The evidence for a round earth was not new in 1492; in fact, Eratosthenes, an Alexandrian geographer who lived nearly sixteen centuries before Columbus's voyage (275-195 B.C.), actually developed a method for calculating the circumference of the earth that is still in use today.
   IV. Eratosthenes's method was correct, but his result—28,700 miles—was about 15 percent too high, probably because of the inaccurate ancient methods of keeping time, and because Aswan was not due south of Alexandria, as Eratosthenes had believed.
   V. When Christopher Columbus sailed across the Atlantic Ocean for the first time in 1492, there were still some people in the world who ignored scientific evidence and believed that the earth was flat, rather than round.
   The BEST order is:
   A. I, II, V, III, IV   B. V, III, IV, I, II   C. V, III, I, II, IV   D. III, V, I, II, IV

17.____

18.
   I. The first name for the child is considered a trial naming, often impersonal and neutral, such as the Ngoni name *Chabwera*, meaning "it has arrived."
   II. This sort of name is not due to any parental indifference to the child, but is a kind of silent recognition of Africa's sometimes high infant death rate; most parents ease the pain of losing a child with the belief that it is not really a person until it has been given a final name.
   III. In many tribal African societies, families often give two different names to their children, at different periods in time.
   IV. After the trial naming period has subsided and it is clear that the child will survive, the parents choose a final name for the child, an act that symbolically completes the act of birth.

18.____

V. In fact, some African first-given names are explicitly uncomplimentary, translating as "I am dead" or "I am ugly," in order to avoid the jealousy of ancestral spirits who might wish to take a child that is especially healthy or attractive.

The BEST order is:
A. III, I, II, V, IV
B. III, IV, II, I, V
C. IV, III, I, II, V
D. IV, V, III, I, II

19. I. Though uncertain of the definite reasons for this behavior, scientists believe the birds digest the clay in order to counteract toxins contained in the seeds of certain fruits that are eaten by macaws.
II. For example, all macaws flock to riverbanks at certain times of the year to eat the clay that is found in river mud.
III. The macaws of South America are not only among the largest and most beautifully colored of the world's flying birds, but they are also one of the smartest.
IV. It is believed that macaws are forced to resort to these toxic fruits during the dry season, when foods are more scarce.
V. The macaw's intelligence has led to intense study by scientists, who have discovered some macaw behaviors that have not yet been explained.

The BEST order is:
A. III, IV, I, II, V
B. III, V, II, I, IV
C. V, II, I, IV, III
D. IV, I, II, III, V

20. I. Although Maggie Kuhn has since passed away, the Gray Panthers are still waging a campaign to reinstate the historical view of the elderly as people whose experience allows them to make their greatest contribution in their later years.
II. In 1972, an elderly woman named Maggie Kuhn responded to this sort of treatment by forming a group called the Gray Panthers, an organization of both old and young adults with the common goal of creating change.
III. This attitude is reflected strongly in the way elderly people are treated by our society; many are forced into early retirement, or are placed in rest homes in which they are isolated from their communities.
IV. Unlike most other cultures around the world, Americans tend to look upon old age with a sense of dread and sadness.
V. Kuhn believed that when the elderly are forced to withdraw into lives that lack purpose, society loses one of its greatest resources: people who have a lifetime of experience and wisdom to offer their communities.

The BEST order is:
A. IV, III, II, V, I
B. IV, II, I, III, V
C. II, IV, III, V, I
D. II, I, IV, III, V

21. I. The current theory among most anthropologists is that humans evolved from apes who lived in trees near the grasslands of Africa.
II. Still, some anthropologists insist that such an invention was necessary for the survival of early humans, and point to the Kung Bushmen of central Africa as a society in which the sling is still used in this way.
III. Two of these inventions—fire, and weapons such as spears and clubs—were obvious defenses against predators, and there is archaeological evidence to support the theory of their use.

IV. Once people had evolved enough to leave the safety of trees and walk upright, they needed the protection of several inventions in order to survive.
V. But another invention, a feather or fiber sling that allowed mothers to carry children while leaving their hands free to gather roots or berries, would certainly have decomposed and left behind no trace of itself.

The BEST order is:
A. I, II, III, V, IV B. IV, I, II, III, V C. I, IV, III, V, II D. IV, III, V, II, I

22.
I. The person holding the bird should keep it in hot water up to its neck, and the person cleaning should work a mild solution of dishwashing liquid into the bird's plumage, paying close attention to the head and neck.
II. When rinsing the bird, after all the oil has been removed, the running water should be directed against the lay of its feathers, until water begins to bead off the surface of the feathers—a sign that all the detergent has been rinsed out.
III. If you have rescued a sea bird from an oil spill and want to restore it to clean and normal living, you need a large sink, a constant supply of running hot water (a little over 100°F), and regular dishwashing liquid.
IV. This cleaning with detergent solution should be repeated as many times as it takes to remove all traces of oil from the bird's feathers, sometime over a period of several days.
V. But before you begin to clean the bird, you must find a partner because cleaning an oiled bird is a two-person job.

The BEST order is:
A. III, I, II, IV, V B. III, V, I, IV, II C. III, I, IV, V, II D. III, IV, V, I, II

22.____

23.
I. The most difficult time of year for the Tsaatang is the spring calving, when the reindeer leave their wintering ground and rush to their accustomed calving place, without stopping by night or by day.
II. Reindeer travel in herds, and though some animals are tamed by the Tsaatang for riding or milking, the herds are allowed to roam free.
III. This journey is hard for the Tsaatang, who carry all their possessions with them, but once it's over it proves worthwhile; the Tsaatang can immediately begin to gather milk from reindeer cows who have given birth.
IV. The Tsaatang, a small tribe who live in the far northwest corner of Mongolia, practice a lifestyle that is completely dependent on the reindeer, their main resource for food, clothing, and transport.
V. The people must follow their yearly migrations, living in portable shelters that resemble Native American tepees.

The BEST order is:
A. I, III, II, V, IV B. I, IV, II, V, III C. IV, I, III, V, II D. IV II, V, I, III

23.____

24.
I. The Romans later improved this system by installing these heated pipe networks throughout walls and ceilings, supplying heat to even the uppermost floors of a building—a system that, to this day, hasn't been much improved.
II. Air-conditioning, the method by which humans control indoor temperatures, was practiced much earlier than most people think.

24.____

III. The earliest heating devices other than open fires were used in 350 B.C. by the ancient Greeks, who directed air that had been heated by underground fires into baked clay pipes that ran under the floor.
IV. Ironically, the first successful cooling system, patented in England in 1831, used fire as its main energy source—fires were lit in the attic of a building, creating an updraft of air that drew cool air into the building through ducts that had underground openings near the river Thames.
V. Cooling buildings was more of a challenge, and wasn't attempted until 1500: a water-based system, designed by Leonardo da Vinci, does not appear to have been successful, since it was never used again.

The BEST order is:
   A. III, V, IV, I, II   B. III, I, II, V, IV   C. II, III, I, V, IV   D. IV, II, III, I, V

25. I. Cold, dry air from Canada passes over the Rocky Mountains and sweeps down onto the plains, where it collides with warm, moist air from the waters of the Gulf of Mexico, and when the two air masses meet, the resulting disturbance sometimes forms a violent funnel cloud that strikes the earth and destroys virtually everything in its path.
II. Hurricanes, storms which are generally not this violent and last much longer, are usually given names by meteorologists, but this tradition cannot be applied to tornados, which have a life span measured in minutes and disappear in the same way as they are born—unnamed.
III. A tornado funnel forms rotating columns of air whose speed reaches three hundred miles an hour—a speed that can only be estimated, because no wind-measuring devices in the direct path of a storm have ever survived.
IV. The natural phenomena known as tornados occur primarily over the Midwestern grasslands of the United States.
V. It is here, meteorologists tell us, that conditions for the formation of tornados are sometimes perfect during the spring months.

The BEST order is:
   A. II IV, V, I, III   B. II, III, I, V, IV   C. IV, V, I, III, II   D. IV, III, I, V, II

25.____

KEY (CORRECT ANSWERS)

1. C
2. C
3. B
4. A
5. B

6. D
7. C
8. D
9. A
10. C

11. B
12. A
13. D
14. B
15. A

16. D
17. C
18. A
19. B
20. A

21. C
22. B
23. D
24. C
25. C

PREPARING WRITTEN MATERIALS

EXAMINATION SECTION
TEST 1

DIRECTIONS: Each of the two sentences in the following questions may contain errors in punctuation, capitalization, or grammar.
If there is an error in only Sentence I, mark your answer A. If there is an error in only Sentence II, mark your answer B.
If there is an error in both Sentence I and Sentence II, mark your answer C. If both Sentence I and II are correct, mark your answer D.
PRINT THE LETTER OF THE CORRECT ANSWER IN THE SPACE AT THE RIGHT.

1. I. The task of typing these reports is to be divided equally between you and me. 1.____
   II. If it was he, I would use a different method for filing these records.

2. I. The new clerk is just as capable as some of the older employees, if not more capable. 2.____
   II. Using his knowledge of arithmetic to check the calculation, the supervisor found no errors in the report.

3. I. A typist who does consistently superior work probably merits promotion. 3.____
   II. In its report on the stenographic unit, the committee pointed out that neither the stenographers nor the typists were adequately trained.

4. I. Entering the office, the desk was noticed immediately by the visitor. 4.____
   II. Arrangements have been made to give this training to whoever applies for it.

5. I. The office manager estimates that this assignment, which is to be handled by you and I, will require about two weeks for completion. 5.____
   II. One of the recommendations of the report is that these kind of forms be discarded because they are of no value.

6. I. The supervisor knew that the typist was a quiet, cooperative, efficient, employee. 6.____
   II. The duties of stenographer are to take dictation notes at conferences and transcribing them.

7. I. The stenographer has learned that she, as well as two typists, is being assigned to the new unit. 7.____
   II. We do not know who you have designated to take charge of the new program.

8. I. He asked, "When do you expect to return?" 8.____
   II. I doubt whether this system will be successful here; it is not suitable for the work of our agency.

119

9. I. It is a policy of this agency to encourage punctuality as a good habit for we employees to adopt.
   II. The successful completion of the task was due largely to them cooperating effectively with the supervisor.

9.____

10. I. Mr. Smith, who is a very competent executive has offered his services to our department.
    II. Every one of the stenographers who work in this office is considered trustworthy.

10.____

11. I. It is very annoying to have a pencil sharpener, which is not in proper working order.
    II. The building watchman checked the door of Charlie's office and found that the lock has been jammed.

11.____

12. I. Since he went on the New York City council a year ago, one of his primary concerns has been safety in the streets.
    II. After waiting in the doorway for about 15 minutes, a black sedan appeared.

12.____

13. I. When you are studying a good textbook is important.
    II. He said he would divide the money equally between you and me.

13.____

14. I. The question is, "How can a large number of envelopes be sealed rapidly without the use of sealing machine?"
    II. The administrator assigned two stenographers, Mary and I, to the new bureau.

14.____

15. I. A dictionary, in addition to the office management textbooks, were placed on his desk.
    II. The concensus of opinion is that none of the employees should be required to work overtime.

15.____

16. I. Mr. Granger has demonstrated that he is as courageous, if not more courageous, than Mr. Brown.
    II. The successful completion of the project depends on the manager's accepting our advisory opinion.

16.____

17. I. Mr. Ames was in favor of issuing a set of rules and regulations for all of us employees to follow.
    II. It is inconceivable that the new clerk knows how to deal with that kind of correspondence.

17.____

18. I. The revised referrence manual is to be used by all of the employees.
    II. Mr. Johnson told Miss Kent and me to accumulate all the letters that we receive.

18.____

19. I. The supervisor said, that before any changes would be made in the attendance report, there must be ample justification for them.
    II. Each of them was asked to amend their preliminary report.

19.____

20. I. Mrs. Peters conferred with Mr. Roberts before she laid the papers on his desk.
    II. As far as this report is concerned, Mr. Williams always has and will be responsible for its preparation.

KEY (CORRECT ANSWERS)

1.	B	11.	C
2.	D	12.	C
3.	D	13.	A
4.	A	14.	B
5.	C	15.	C
6.	C	16.	A
7.	B	17.	B
8.	D	18.	A
9.	C	19.	C
10.	A	20.	B

TEST 2

DIRECTIONS: Each question or incomplete statement is followed by several suggested answers or completions. Select the one that BEST answers the question or completes the statement. *PRINT THE LETTER OF THE CORRECT ANSWER IN THE SPACE AT THE RIGHT.*

Questions 1-9.

DIRECTIONS: Questions 1 through 9 consist of pairs of sentences which may or may not contain errors in grammar, capitalization, or punctuation.
If both sentences are correct, mark your answer A.
If the first sentence only is correct, mark your answer B.
If the second sentence only is correct, mark your answer C.
If both sentences are incorrect, mark your answer D.
NOTE: Consider a sentence correct if it contains no errors, although there may be other correct ways of writing the sentence.

1. I. An unusual conference will be held today at George Washington high school.   1.____
   II. The principal of the school, Dr. Pace, described the meeting as "a unique opportunity for educators to exchange ideas.

2. I. Studio D, which they would ordinarily use, will be occupied at that time.   2.____
   II. Any other studio, which is properly equipped, may be used instead.

3. I. D.H. Lawrence's <u>Sons and Lovers</u> were discussed on today's program.   3.____
   II. Either Eliot's or Yeats's work is to be covered next week.

4. I. This program is on the air for three years now, and has a well-established audience.   4.____
   II. We have received many complimentary letters from listeners, and scarcely no critical ones.

5. I. Both Mr. Owen and Mr. Mitchell have addressed the group.   5.____
   II. As has Mr. Stone, whose talks have been especially well received.

6. I. The original program was different in several respects from the version that eventually went on the air.   6.____
   II. Each of the three announcers who Mr. Scott thought had had suitable experience was asked whether he would be willing to take on the special assignment.

7. I. A municipal broadcasting system provides extensive coverage of local events, but also reports national and international news.   7.____
   II. A detailed account of happenings in the South may be carried by a local station hundreds of miles away.

8. I. Jack Doe the announcer and I will be working on the program.   8.____
   II. The choice of musical selections has been left up to he and I.

9. I. Mr. Taylor assured us that "he did not anticipate any difficulty in making arrangements for the broadcast."
    II. Although there had seemed at first to be certain problems; these had been solved.

Questions 10-14.

DIRECTIONS: Questions 10 through 14 consist of pairs of sentences which may contain errors in grammar, sentence structure, punctuation, or spelling, or both sentences may be correct. Consider a sentence correct if it contains no errors, although there may be other correct ways of writing the sentence.
If only Sentence I contains an error, mark your answer A.
If only Sentence II contains an error, mark your answer B.
If both sentences contain errors, mark your answer C.
If both sentences are correct, mark your answer D.

10. I. No employee considered to be indispensable will be assigned to the new office.
    II. The arrangement of the desks and chairs give the office a neat appearance.

11. I. The recommendation, accompanied by a report, was delivered this morning.
    II. Mr. Green thought the procedure would facilitate his work; he knows better now.

12. I. Limiting the term "property" to tangible property, in the criminal mischief setting, accords with prior case law holding that only tangible property came within the purview of the offense of malicious mischief.
    II. Thus, a person who intentionally destroys the property of another, but under an honest belief that he has title to such property, cannot be convicted of criminal mischief under the Revised Penal Law.

13. I. Very early in its history, New York enacted statutes from time to time punishing, either as a felony or as a misdemeanor, malicious injuries to various kinds of property: piers, booms, dams, bridges, etc.
    II. The application of the statute is necessarily restricted to trespassory takings with larcenous intent: namely with intent permanently or virtually permanently to "appropriate" property or "deprive" the owner of its use.

14. I. Since the former Penal Law did not define the instruments of forgery in a general fashion, its crime of forgery was held to be narrower than the common law offense in this respect and to embrace only those instruments explicitly specified in the substantive provisions.
    II. After entering the barn through an open door for the purpose of stealing, it was closed by the defendants.

Questions 15-20.

DIRECTIONS: Questions 15 through 20 consist of pairs of sentences which may or may not contain errors in grammar, capitalization, or punctuation.
If both sentences are correct, mark your answer A.
If the first sentence only is correct, mark your answer B.
If the second sentence only is correct, mark your answer C.
If both sentences are incorrect, mark your answer D.
NOTE: Consider a sentence correct if it contains no errors, although there may be other ways of writing the sentence.

15. I. The program, which is currently most popular, is a news broadcast.
    II. The engineer assured his supervisor that there was no question of his being late again.

16. I. The announcer recommended that the program originally scheduled for that time be cancelled.
    II. Copies of the script may be given to whoever is interested.

17. I. A few months ago it looked like we would be able to broadcast the concert live.
    II. The program manager, as well as the announcers, were enthusiastic about the plan.

18. I. No speaker on the subject of education is more interesting than he.
    II. If he would have had the time, we would have scheduled him for a regular weekly broadcast.

19. I. This quartet, in its increasingly complex variations on a simple theme, admirably illustrates Professor Baker's point.
    II. Listeners interested in these kind of ideas will find his recently published study of Haydn rewarding.

20. I. The Commissioner's resignation at the end of next month marks the end of a long public service career.
    II. Outstanding among his numerous achievements were his successful implementation of several revolutionary schemes to reorganize the agency.

KEY (CORRECT ANSWERS)

1.	C	11.	D
2.	B	12.	C
3.	C	13.	B
4.	D	14.	A
5.	B	15.	C
6.	A	16.	A
7.	A	17.	D
8.	D	18.	B
9.	D	19.	B
10.	B	20.	B

PREPARING WRITTEN MATERIAL
EXAMINATION SECTION
TEST 1

DIRECTIONS: Each of the sentences in this test may be classified under one of the following four categories:
- A. Faulty because of incorrect grammar or word usage
- B. Faulty because of incorrect punctuation
- C. Faulty because of incorrect capitalization or incorrect spelling
- D. Correct

Examine each sentence carefully to determine under which of the above four options it is best classified. Then, in the space to the right, print the capital letter preceding the option which is the BEST of the four suggested above. (Note that each faulty sentence contains but one type of error. Consider a sentence to be correct if it contains none of the types of errors mentioned, even though there may be other correct ways of expressing the same thought.)

1. He sent the notice to the clerk who you hired yesterday.   1.____

2. It must be admitted, however that you were not informed of this change.   2.____

3. Only the employee who have served in this grade for at least two years are eligible for promotion.   3.____

4. The work was divided equally between she and Mary.   4.____

5. He thought that you were not available at that time.   5.____

6. When the messenger returns; please give him this package.   6.____

7. The new secretary prepared, typed, addressed, and delivered, the notices.   7.____

8. Walking into the room, his desk can be seen at the rear.   8.____

9. Although John has worked here longer than She, he produces a smaller amount of work.   9.____

10. She said she could of typed this report yesterday.   10.____

11. Neither one of these procedures are adequate for the efficient performance of this task.   11.____

12. The typewriter is the tool of the typist; the cash register, the tool of the cashier.   12.____

2 (#1)

13. "The assignment must be completed as soon as possible" said the supervisor. 13.____

14. As you know, office handbooks are issued to all new Employees. 14.____

15. Writing a speech is sometimes easier than to deliver it before an audience. 15.____

16. Mr. Brown our accountant, will audit the accounts next week. 16.____

17. Give the assignment to whomever is able to do it most efficiently. 17.____

18. The supervisor expected either your or I to file these reports. 18.____

KEY (CORRECT ANSWERS)

1.	A	11.	A
2.	B	12.	C
3.	D	13.	B
4.	A	14.	C
5.	D	15.	A
6.	B	16.	B
7.	B	17.	A
8.	A	18.	A
9.	C		
10.	A		

TEST 2

DIRECTIONS: Each of the sentences in this test may be classified under one of the following four categories:
  A. Faulty because of incorrect grammar or word usage
  B. Faulty because of incorrect punctuation
  C. Faulty because of incorrect capitalization or incorrect spelling
  D. Correct

Examine each sentence carefully to determine under which of the above four options it is best classified. Then, in the space to the right, print the capital letter preceding the option which is the BEST of the four suggested above. (Note that each faulty sentence contains but one type of error. Consider a sentence to be correct if it contains none of the types of errors mentioned, even though there may be other correct ways of expressing the same thought.)

1. The fire apparently started in the storeroom, which is usually locked.   1.____

2. On approaching the victim, two bruises were noticed by this officer.   2.____

3. The officer, who was there examined the report with great care.   3.____

4. Each employee in the office had a seperate desk.   4.____

5. All employees including members of the clerical staff, were invited to the lecture. 5.____

6. The suggested Procedure is similar to the one now in use.   6.____

7. No one was more pleased with the new procedure than the chauffeur.   7.____

8. He tried to persaude her to change the procedure.   8.____

9. The total of the expenses charged to petty cash were high.   9.____

10. An understanding between him and I was finally reached.   10.____

KEY (CORRECT ANSWERS)

1.	D	6.	C
2.	A	7.	D
3.	B	8.	C
4.	C	9.	A
5.	B	10.	A

TEST 3

DIRECTIONS: Each of the sentences in this test may be classified under one of the following four categories:
- A. Faulty because of incorrect grammar or word usage
- B. Faulty because of incorrect punctuation
- C. Faulty because of incorrect capitalization or incorrect spelling
- D. Correct

Examine each sentence carefully to determine under which of the above four options it is best classified. Then, in the space to the right, print the capital letter preceding the option which is the BEST of the four suggested above. (Note that each faulty sentence contains but one type of error. Consider a sentence to be correct if it contains none of the types of errors mentioned, even though there may be other correct ways of expressing the same thought.)

1. They told both he and I that the prisoner had escaped. 1._____

2. Any superior officer, who, disregards the just complaint of his subordinates, is remiss in the performance of his duty. 2._____

3. Only those members of the national organization who resided in the Middle West attended the conference in Chicago. 3._____

4. We told him to give the national organization assignment to whoever was available. 4._____

5. Please do not disappoint and embarass us by not appearing in court. 5._____

6. Although the office's speech proved to be entertaining, the topic was not relevent to the main theme of the conference. 6._____

7. In February all new officers attended a training course in which they were learned in their principal duties and the fundamental operating procedure of the department. 7._____

8. I personally seen inmate Jones threaten inmates Smith and Green with bodily harm if they refused to participate in the plot. 8._____

9. To the layman, who on a chance visit to the prison observes everything functioning smoothly, the maintenance of prison discipline may seem to be a relatively easily realizable objective. 9._____

10. The prisoners in cell block fourty were forbidden to sit on the cell cots during the recreation hour. 10._____

KEY (CORRECT ANSWERS)

1.	A	6.	C
2.	B	7.	A
3.	C	8.	A
4.	D	9.	D
5.	C	10.	C

TEST 4

DIRECTIONS: Each of the sentences in this test may be classified under one of the following four categories:
- A. Faulty because of incorrect grammar or word usage
- B. Faulty because of incorrect punctuation
- C. Faulty because of incorrect capitalization or incorrect spelling
- D. Correct

Examine each sentence carefully to determine under which of the above four options it is best classified. Then, in the space to the right, print the capital letter preceding the option which is the BEST of the four suggested above. (Note that each faulty sentence contains but one type of error. Consider a sentence to be correct if it contains none of the types of errors mentioned, even though there may be other correct ways of expressing the same thought.)

1. I cannot encourage you any. 1.____
2. You always look well in those sort of clothes. 2.____
3. Shall we go to the park? 3.____
4. The man whome he introduced was Mr. Carey. 4.____
5. She saw the letter laying here this morning. 5.____
6. It should rain before the Afternoon is over. 6.____
7. They have already went home. 7.____
8. That Jackson will be elected is evident. 8.____
9. He does not hardly approve of us. 9.____
10. It was he, who won the prize. 10.____

KEY (CORRECT ANSWERS)

1. A   6. C
2. A   7. A
3. D   8. D
4. C   9. A
5. A   10. B

TEST 5

DIRECTIONS: Each of the sentences in this test may be classified under one of the following four categories:
  A. Faulty because of incorrect grammar or word usage
  B. Faulty because of incorrect punctuation
  C. Faulty because of incorrect capitalization or incorrect spelling
  D. Correct

Examine each sentence carefully to determine under which of the above four options it is best classified. Then, in the space to the right, print the capital letter preceding the option which is the BEST of the four suggested above. (Note that each faulty sentence contains but one type of error. Consider a sentence to be correct if it contains none of the types of errors mentioned, even though there may be other correct ways of expressing the same thought.)

1. Shall we go to the park. 1.____

2. They are, alike, in this particular way. 2.____

3. They gave the poor man sume food when he knocked on the door. 3.____

4. I regret the loss caused by the error. 4.____

5. The students' will have a new teacher. 5.____

6. They sweared to bring out all the facts. 6.____

7. He decided to open a branch store on 33rd street. 7.____

8. His speed is equal and more than that of a racehorse. 8.____

9. He felt very warm on that Summer day. 9.____

10. He was assisted by his friend, who lives in the next house. 10.____

KEY (CORRECT ANSWERS)

1.	B	6.	A
2.	B	7.	C
3.	C	8.	A
4.	D	9.	C
5.	B	10.	D

TEST 6

DIRECTIONS: Each of the sentences in this test may be classified under one of the following four categories:
- A. Faulty because of incorrect grammar or word usage
- B. Faulty because of incorrect punctuation
- C. Faulty because of incorrect capitalization or incorrect spelling
- D. Correct

Examine each sentence carefully to determine under which of the above four options it is best classified. Then, in the space to the right, print the capital letter preceding the option which is the BEST of the four suggested above. (Note that each faulty sentence contains but one type of error. Consider a sentence to be correct if it contains none of the types of errors mentioned, even though there may be other correct ways of expressing the same thought.)

1. The climate of New York is colder than California. 1.____
2. I shall wait for you on the corner. 2.____
3. Did we see the boy who, we think, is the leader. 3.____
4. Being a modest person, John seldom talks about his invention. 4.____
5. The gang is called the smith street bos. 5.____
6. He seen the man break into the store. 6.____
7. We expected to lay still there for quite a while. 7.____
8. He is considered to be the Leader of his organization. 8.____
9. Although I recieved an invitation, I won't go. 9.____
10. The letter must be here some place. 10.____

KEY (CORRECT ANSWERS)

1. A   6. A
2. D   7. A
3. B   8. C
4. D   9. C
5. C   10. A

TEST 7

DIRECTIONS: Each of the sentences in this test may be classified under one of the following four categories:
   A. Faulty because of incorrect grammar or word usage
   B. Faulty because of incorrect punctuation
   C. Faulty because of incorrect capitalization or incorrect spelling
   D. Correct

Examine each sentence carefully to determine under which of the above four options it is best classified. Then, in the space to the right, print the capital letter preceding the option which is the BEST of the four suggested above. (Note that each faulty sentence contains but one type of error. Consider a sentence to be correct if it contains none of the types of errors mentioned, even though there may be other correct ways of expressing the same thought.)

1. I though it to be he. 1._____
2. We expect to remain here for a long time. 2._____
3. The committee was agreed. 3._____
4. Two-thirds of the building are finished. 4._____
5. The water was froze. 5._____
6. Everyone of the salesmen must supply their own car. 6._____
7. Who is the author of Gone With the Wind? 7._____
8. He marched on and declaring that he would never surrender. 8._____
9. Who shall I say called? 9._____
10. Everyone has left but they. 10._____

KEY (CORRECT ANSWERS)

1.	A	6.	A
2.	D	7.	B
3.	D	8.	A
4.	A	9.	D
5.	A	10.	D

TEST 8

DIRECTIONS: Each of the sentences in this test may be classified under one of the following four categories:
- A. Faulty because of incorrect grammar or word usage
- B. Faulty because of incorrect punctuation
- C. Faulty because of incorrect capitalization or incorrect spelling
- D. Correct

Examine each sentence carefully to determine under which of the above four options it is best classified. Then, in the space to the right, print the capital letter preceding the option which is the BEST of the four suggested above. (Note that each faulty sentence contains but one type of error. Consider a sentence to be correct if it contains none of the types of errors mentioned, even though there may be other correct ways of expressing the same thought.)

1. Who did we give the order to?
2. Send your order in immediately.
3. I believe I paid the Bill.
4. I have not met but one person.
5. Why aren't Tom, and Fred, going to the dance?
6. What reason is there for him not going?
7. The seige of Malta was a tremendous event.
8. I was there yesterday I assure you
9. Your ukulele is better than mine.
10. No one was there only Mary.

KEY (CORRECT ANSWERS)

1. A
2. D
3. C
4. A
5. B
6. A
7. C
8. B
9. C
10. A

TEST 9

DIRECTIONS: In each of the following groups of sentences, one of the four sentences is faulty in grammar, punctuation, or capitalization. Select the INCORRECT sentence in each case.

1. A. If you had stood at home and done your homework, you would not have failed in arithmetic.
    B. Her affected manner annoyed every member of the audience.
    C. How will the new law affect our income taxes?
    D. The plants were not affected by the long, cold winter, but they succumbed to the drought of summer.

    1.____

2. A. He is one of the most able men who have been in the Senate.
    B. It is he who is to blame for the lamentable mistake.
    C. Haven't you a helpful suggestion to make at this time?
    D. The money was robbed from the blind man's cup.

    2.____

3. A. The amount of children in this school is steadily increasing.
    B. After taking an apple from the table, she went out to play.
    C. He borrowed a dollar from me.
    D. I had hoped my brother would arrive before me.

    3.____

4. A. Whom do you think I hear from every week?
    B. Who do you think is the right man for the job?
    C. Who do you think I found in the room?
    D. He is the man whom we considered a good candidate for the presidency.

    4.____

5. A. Quietly the puppy laid down before the fireplace.
    B. You have made your bed; now lie in it.
    C. I was badly sunburned because I had lain too long in the sun.
    D. I laid the doll on the bed and left the room.

    5.____

KEY (CORRECT ANSWERS)

1. A
2. D
3. A
4. C
5. A

www.ingramcontent.com/pod-product-compliance
Lightning Source LLC
Chambersburg PA
CBHW082207300426
44117CB00016B/2697